OXFORD
DAYS

ALSO BY PAUL WEST

FICTION

A Cupboard for the Sun
A Fifth of November
O.K.
The Dry Danube
Life with Swan
Terrestrials
Sporting with Amaryllis
The Tent of Orange Mist
Love's Mansion
The Women of Whitechapel and Jack the Ripper
Lord Byron's Doctor
The Place in Flowers Where Pollen Rests
The Universe, and Other Fictions
Rat Man of Paris
The Very Rich Hours of Count von Stauffenberg
Gala
Colonel Mint
Caliban's Filibuster
Bela Lugosi's White Christmas
I'm Expecting to Live Quite Soon
Alley Jaggers
Tenement of Clay

NONFICTION

Master Class
The Secret Lives of Words
My Mother's Music
A Stroke of Genius
Sheer Fiction—Volumes I, II, III
Portable People
Out of My Depths: A Swimmer in the Universe
Words for a Deaf Daughter
I, Said the Sparrow
The Wine of Absurdity
The Snow Leopard
The Modern Novel
Byron and the Spoiler's Art
James Ensor

Paul West at Oxford

For Alastair,
Visions, or ramblings, of
the red stamping-ground
and those dreaming choirs!

OXFORD
an inclination
DAYS

PAUL WEST

Warmest regards,

Paul
2002

BRITISH AMERICAN PUBLISHING, LTD.

LATHAM, NEW YORK

Published by British American Publishing, Ltd.
4 British American Boulevard
Latham, New York 12110

Printed in the United States of America

ISBN (cloth): 0-945167-52-0

Library of Congress Cataloging-in-Publication Data

West, Paul, date.
  Oxford days : an inclination / by Paul West.
    p. cm.
  ISBN 0-945167-52-0 (alk. paper)

  1. West, Paul, date—Homes and haunts—England—Oxford. 2.
Novelists, American—20th century—Biography. 3. University of
Oxford—Students—Biography. 4. Oxford (England)—Social life and
customs. 5. Americans—England—Oxford. I. Title.
  PS3573.E8247 Z466 2002
  813'.54—dc21
                    2001007498

To Bryan and Janette

the immensity of the here and now

—Hermann Broch, *The Death of Virgil*

CONTENTS

1
MY SWEET TOMORROW

2
"UP"

3
SEZ

4
TRAPPINGS

5
IDEAS

1

MY SWEET TOMORROW

RENISHAW

It was rumored that if any of us in our uncouth way presented himself at the doors of the Sitwells' Renishaw Hall, begging a penny for the Guy (effigy of the Gunpowder Plotter Guy Fawkes) or simply pleading for a leftover crust or two, or even "a drink of water, Mester," Sir Osbert or his minions would send us away calling us all *Mellors*, after the plebeian upstart of D. H. Lawrence's novel *Lady Chatterley's Lover*, set in this very village (and one other). When I myself showed up hoping for her and not him (Dame Edith rather than Sir Osbert, the poet rather than the autobiographer), he never said *Mellors* at all.

"So you write, young feller-me-lad."

"Yes sir, I do. Stories."

"Committing pen to paper."

"Yes, sir, but—"

"Ah, but not often."

"From time to time, sir."

"Thank God for that. How may I disappoint you?"

"Well, sir, I wondered—"

"I never help, I never advise, boy. Are you Jewish?"

I told him no, but I would have answered no to anything. Was I an Assyrian, Kurdish, Cypriot? I had little idea of what he meant.

"Well, good, that's a blessing. So you write. Well, don't. Whatever form the disease takes with you, resist it and get a decent job mining coal."

He hadn't even asked to see the sheaf of twaddle I'd brought with me, rolled up like certificates. He hadn't identified me as the genius I hoped I was. His own prose, like his speech, was spattered with single dashes—not dashes in pairs—and, although I thought his *Left Hand, Right Hand* a plausible theory of personality (the left's palmistry is the givens, the right's what you've made of them), I had never thought him a convincing theorist. I just wanted a sign from above that all was going well. I was sixteen and rather helpless. Who on earth, what prankster, had put me up to this, fessing my fetish at the portals of well-to-do aristos?

His sister's response, when I showed up a year later to ask her to judge a poetry contest (she agreed), was entirely different. At once she engaged the future for me, spelling out answers to questions I had never intended asking. She read my superego like a book, insisting that of course I should try for Oxford, where they trained prime ministers and taught you how to drink brandy and get plump, whereas Cambridge was for those awful scientists or boffins, back-room boys, who wanted to blow the world up. She mentioned *The Shadow of Cain*, which I had actually read.

"Oxford," she said mesmerizingly, "will make you reach beyond yourself and be something in this world, the other place will stand you, dear boy, at a microscope and send you blind. I never attended a university myself. My nose was so hideous they decided to keep me out of sight in the hall cupboard. At least until some doctor, not a Nazi, made me presentable and straightened my dear old Plantagenet schnoz straight. You take those exams, and don't let me catch you not doing well. Tell them you know me and that I have taught you to appreciate poetry."

"Well, you have, miss." I had read her extraordinary patient look at the texture of Alexander Pope, a most unusual book for its period, with all the virtues of F. R. Leavis's close reading without his moral bigotry.

She was shocked, yet stubbornly gratified.

"No science, young you."

"No, ma'am. I promise. I can't count anyway."

"*Oxford.*"

"Oxford, ma'am, if I can."

"Of course you can. If you don't, they'll hear from me. There are some awfully nasty people in the literary profession, young you, and they are going to hear from *me*, vulgarly known as getting it in the neck." Or from Maynard Hollingsworth the estate agent who swept through the village in gaiters, braying and barking, his demeanor one of irascible gentility. When he bowed, some internal mercury tilted free of its vacuum and silvered his track behind him.

A loose god had walked among us, urgent and aloof. Would even he have said *Mellors* except as a curse under his beery breath?

Perhaps the most incongruous part of my childhood and adolescence was the way in which, unnoticed by me, various creative and cultural worthies—icons even—sauntered with the Sitwells through the village streets of Eckington, stopping at this or that pub for a drink. Here came Alec and Merula Guinness, the painter John Piper, the composer William Walton, the poet Dylan Thomas (virtually adopted and protected by Edith), and several others, an aesthetic invasion unidentified by locals who regarded them as mere "nobs" come slumming. With them, I vaguely recall, came Osbert's constant friend Captain Stanier, one of those who held on to and exploited his rank after the First War. The teenager who saw them without heeding them was planning his exit into, he hoped, their company, faintly marveling at the facile way the Sitwells arranged for a couple of railway companies (the London-Midland-Scottish mainly) to put on a special train to whisk these luminaries from London up to the Renishaw halt. Money, plus grace and favor, swung that, I imagine; after all, the world was the Sitwells' oyster, they who spent much of the year in a castle in Italy, or in a mansion on the east coast at Scarborough. I imagine now that W. H. Auden and Aldous Huxley used to put in an appearance in Lady Chatterley's village until they lit out for the United States.

Had I realized, what on earth would I have said, butting in with my "I too"s in the village street, chronically unaware that the world I longed to join had several times strolled past the aspidistra in our music-room window. I should have been more alert to the way these unselfconscious artists argued in the street, heedless of traffic or villagers, almost a grown-up version of the schoolboys from Spinkhill College, the Catholic establishment high on a hill not far away, whose boys trickled into our streets on Saturday afternoons to buy candies and cookies. I think I once saw Dylan Thomas, untidy moppet, pausing in front of the tripe shop, afflicted with a complex rune the Brit reviewers would scold him for. But I was only just waking up, so to speak, coming to ambitious life, after a long and fruitful sleep in which, I distinctly recall, I had a recurring dream of reading, yet reading too slowly for all I wanted it to do for me, and therefore in a preparatory panic. How ironic to have had such illustrious visitations while gestating, pecking through the shell with my literary beak. First the Romans, so long ago, then the Norse and the French, and then the illuminati of London lent invisibly to that village of fact and fable.

THE FRENCH

Dazzle them, said my mentors at school on the eve of my departure to sit the scholarship examinations, almost in the mood of Diaghilev's *"Étonne moi!"* addressed to Jean Cocteau, who was surely capable of just that. Time and again Cocteau shook Diaghilev. Too much of my knowledge was based on rumor, as I found out later, but I did know Rousseau's *Reveries of the Solitary Walker* almost by heart and saw that one of his notions—that of at least being *different*—I must not only take to heart but, during my candidate week, enact with choreographic zeal. It was like being obliged, within the confines of those much-climbed-over ancient college walls, to soar beyond the human race, yet without going too high. If one achieved excessive solar apogee, he would seem better suited to a rest clinic in the provinces than to a court near the Cam or an Isis quad or at worst, a teacher training college where half-wits hard-earned massive parchments to mount on their walls. The main thing, however, was to fly.

"Yes, dazzle them," my mother said, "but give them a good helping of facts too. If you know any. It's no use giving them well-whipped froth. Use the dates of things. Quote what you're talking about. Write things out before you write them into your answer. Try and remember as many details as you can, as if you'd *been* there."

"Where?" I asked her, knowing I was going to flunk.

"Any century you like," she breezily answered. "Or at a certain place in a piece of music." I knew what she meant, but my wayward policeman's mind was more inclined to have noticed the thin, humble rings worn by bank tellers as they shuffled fortunes to and fro over the mahogany.

At a lower level of befuddlement, well below the suicidal masochism of seeming too brilliant to live, there was the near felony of perhaps winning a scholarship for committing crimes which, in a more prosaic ordeal, would get you failed. With nothing to lose and all to gain, I felt like a gambler, more Dostoevskian than Vegas-ian, not even sure that what I was planking down on the light or the dark blue was valid currency at all, but giddily conscious of tempting the fates without getting into debt. The whole test was a lottery, even the winner uncertain of being allocated to the college of his preference, since many colleges examined jointly and then competed among themselves, over the port and walnuts, for the cream.

A solider student than I would have worried about being unable to march his data past the reviewing stand, whereas I, exhorted to twist the questions to my needs, had a field day throughout that initial baptism-of-fire week, sidestepping and weaving, importing irrelevance like ersatz gold leaf, discarding the examination papers themselves, boldly setting and answering (or begging!) questions of my own. My strategy, I now see, was to drive the examiners out of their minds into mine. "Look!" my scribbled voluntaries cried, "*I am here. This* is what I do. Choose me, not them (or me among the few)." After thirty-five writing hours, two interviews, and a return train journey from Cambridge with my swollen suitcase in the tourniquet of my bathrobe's cord, I began the wait. An award would bring a telegram, followed a week later by a one-line listing, precious as lutetium, of my name among others in the better-class newspapers. In the event, I received a letter, in which the master of the college explained that I could not even be admitted as a "commoner," which was Oxbridgese (a hangover from days of bone-deep grace and favor) for entrance unfunded. I had not even been allowed in.

Too tired to think in terms of catastrophe, I leniently heard out my elders, who said it had all been practice; I had not been expected to "pull up any trees," except by some eleventh-hour egregious act of God. Next year I would go again, trying for both universities, but only in English: no more French, which upset me (I preferred its literature to ours, and still do). Back to my books I went, a chastened performing animal, sacrificing Rousseau to Wordsworth, Rabelais to Swift, my innermost mind haunted by that heady sample of the Promised Land, Sidney Sussex College, where Oliver Cromwell had been. I yearned dismally for the flyblown quiet of its coal-smoky rooms (even a candidate had "rooms" and not just a room), the atmospheric snooze of the fire in the grate, the kettle that boiled thereon like a hydraulic ally, the rind-stiff marmalade on the dead toast in the dining hall, the tamed lawns in the courts, the continual bells, the river-sweet fog. It had all gone up in some kind of smoke, or down, like a severed head, into the enormous picnic basket into which one laid one's script when one's best had been done, or the proctor said stop.

"Don't *fret* about it," my mother told me. "Don't *stew*. There's always another chance next year."

She was right, but I didn't want to wait a year. Having all of a sudden formed a taste for the Oxbridge life, I wanted to clinch things then and there.

"Perhaps it was the French," I said.

"Well," my mother said, "just listen to your father on the French, and the Belgians too. You might have been better off with German."

"Oh," I answered, in some such words as these (taking care not to stir her up too much, or we would see bags of sugar hitting the walls and have to dig out the flashlights to go and find her later on): "You mean something tidy and orderly, like the Germans in the stuff I read. I think I'll bank it all on English, a language I seem to know."

"You know some of it," she teased. "Nobody knows all of it; it's huge. *My stars*, it's enormous!"

"Certainly not the Germans or the French or the Belgians," I said. I imagined a language like an iceberg, most of it out of sight and earshot, never used by its speakers. What could you do with such a monster? As much as possible, even if it took another fifty years. My mother and I were being examined together, almost as if in music, she the sorceress, I the prosing toad.

Tully

One could, I discovered, form a crush on a place, on a college's official polychrome scarf, its plumbing, its amber evening lamps. That I had been born for (though not into) all this I had no doubt, and that I had, like the gauche prince of legend, been shut out I could not believe. A god had failed, and also a boy. Imagine my puerile agonizings as, in the spring and summer that followed, I ran into fellow competitors who, as the jargon ran, were "going up" that fall, or, worse, the elect preparing for their second or third year "in residence." I longed to go up, with all that phrase's hint of aerial promotion, and to be in residence would be enclosure in a commodious trance. Furtively, at football or cricket matches, I perused the foreheads of the chosen few, eventually deciding that the typical winner's brow was low, concave, and signed with three undulant creases, whereas my own, impassive mirrors proved, was high, bulged slightly, and bore no lines at all. In a desperate effort to make the mind conform, I incised three magical cicatrices above my eyes with the round end of a nail file, admiring the look of distracted maturity I thought they conferred, until the skin regained its natural tension and I became an also-ran again.

Slogging away at books in my third-story bedroom, at a table to whose overvarnished top my elbows stuck fast, I ran the gamut of affronted aspiration, certain I would glide in automatically next time provided, say, I wore an olive-green shirt, or looked paler than Banquo's ghost. A more pragmatic magic, however, set me poring over paperbound volumes of past examination papers (though I shrank from looking in the back at those in whose presence I had betrayed myself last year). Within those ferro-cyanide-blue covers lay the keys of a genteel kingdom, perhaps in the compulsory translation from Latin (*how* could Tacitus's "*temptat clausa*," bald brace in a museum tongue, mean all of "he tried to open all the closed doors"? Was this to be my own motto, malefically secreted among the stuff of my undoing?). Or was it in the three-hour general essay paper ("Discuss logic," or " 'The unexamined life is not worth having.' Consider.")? Who was I to opine on logic, expert that I was in muddle, especially after grappling with Bertrand Russell's *The Problems of Philosophy*, in which all chairs became unreal fascii of qualities? As for the unexamined life, I knew only, from recent bitter ordeals, that it might actually be an unmitigated joy (no more three-hour essays) and that, in a less shallow sense, although the unexamined life might not be worth having, the examined one might not be worth living.

In nightmares I kept meeting pimply geniuses with narrow, sunken, striated brows, who jubilantly remarked on the easiness of the translation from Chinese, the piece of cake the literary history paper had been (mad minutiae pincered from a continuum rolling from Homer to Haldor Laxness), and the trivial stimulus of even the hardest essay topic ("Discuss any teleology implicit, or seemingly so, in the categorical imperative"). The only consolation, idle gossip of school cloakrooms, was that these examinations were stiffer than the universities' own final degree papers; graduates (oh, what Prometheans!) had repeatedly said so, and the dons (noetic pharaohs) concurred. Almost broken on the wheel when young, the winners breezed through the ensuing three years as if playing snap. Into the bargain, I came from a grammar school (where they syntactically and strategically meant business), and still less a public school, meaning private, which as often as not had closed scholarships available to its own boys only. Besides, *we* had girls on our premises, which surely proved the school's essential lack of high seriousness. I envisioned a hypothetical secondary scholarship, available only to our school, and then dreamed up the deaths—by traffic, pneumonia, and brainstorm—of my immediate rivals, at length accepting my award with the smile of a fireball coming home to roost.

Studying previous papers, those libretti of past inquisitions, I marveled at the arcane trophies to be had. As well as open scholarships, which explained themselves, there were the aforementioned closed ones, restricted to Etonians, descendants of King Canute, or anyone born west of a line drawn from Berwick-on-Tweed to

Land's End, but also indiscreet or painterly sounding exhibitions, wholly enigmatic sizarships with faint connotations of glue or paste, and bisected things called demyships, for which one perhaps received only a half-stipend. Lowest of all were commonerships, at which I now set my cap. Of such illustrious colleges as Cambridge's King's, which may have been only for male royalty, and Trinity, only for the devout or those who thought in threes, or Oxford's Magdalen (what if one whorishly mispronounced it during interview?), and Balliol, which was full of invincibly brilliant Scotsmen who thought all night in calculus, I had no hopes. In fact, I was addressing my endeavors to St. Catherine's and Selwyn Colleges, Cambridge, combined, and St. Edmund Hall, Oxford. Amazing as it now seems, not every college offered an examination in English Literature, almost as if, compared with the intricate preliminaries of Medicine, Literae Humaniores, or what Cambridge forbiddingly termed Moral Sciences, it weren't a serious subject at all. Anyone worth his salt knew it backward and would not persist with anything so ephemeral; but for secondary-school boys it might just do, like them having come so recently into being, an upstart lit, for an upstart lot.

So I forgot Oliver Cromwell's college and, to equip myself with a unique, local angle, began to study the poems of Edith Sitwell. Not daring to present myself again for interview at the portals of haunted Renishaw Hall, I schooled myself in village gossip, amassing gaudy yarns of Edith's ring-encrusted hands, her habit of sleeping in a coffin in ornate robes, her basilisk's eye, her Plantagenet nose like a molten string bean, the iron mask she had been forced to wear as a child. Opening the local flower show on St. Peter's cricket ground, where I had often flung red leather balls at clay-brown stumps, she looked like some hopelessly etiolated macaw, not of this aviary at all but rented for a fee to be paid in Erewhon orchids. Fervently I worked out close analyses of her most sensuous poems, evolving bogus theories (if indeed the expression itself is not tautologous) of verbal enamel and the annular baroque, identifying at a class-conscious distance with her exotic aloofness, and even going so far afield as to rehearse little monologues on Sacheverell Sitwell's poems, Osbert's slapdash use of the dash. A contribution to knowledge it was not, but it *was* viaticum and exam fodder in one. After a few months immersed in *Façade* and *Gold Coast Customs*, our man from Renishaw was ready for the Goliath brains of next December's inquisitors. This time, although the two examinations almost overlapped, there would be no sixteen papers in six days (which had meant three papers on four) but, in either place, a civilized new-style trivium of Authors, Periods, and General, to be followed by an interview, at which one stood a fair chance of being incompletely exhausted. Oxford came first, then I had to go, via Bletchley Junction, where Franz Kafka was reputed to have lived in the signal box, to Cambridge, a tricky cross-country trip: from the patrician matrix of prime ministers to the sagest old clinic of the mid-century.

St. Edmund Hall was a tiny place just off Oxford's thunder-
ous High Street, where University College and others were sub-
siding an inch each year owing to the vibration from traffic and,
some decades thence, would disappear from view into a Dark Ages
compost that no doubt included the bonemeal of Oxford's epony-
mous ox. The formulas of arrival did not vary markedly from
those of what Oxford men referred to, with jocular hauteur, as
"the other place"; yet it was a serious jocularity, and what
Oxford respected in its less fruity sibling was a medieval childhood
held in common. Arriving at the porter's lodge, one was put into
the custody of a "scout," who, presumably knowing his way
through the Mohicans and Comanches of the academy, con-
ducted one to yet another set of temporary rooms, whose absent
tenant had his embossed calling card set in a little brass frame let
into the oak, as the outer door was called. To be private here, for
whatever purpose, you locked the outer door, known as sporting
the oak. Needless to say, I sported mine as soon as I could, and
took out my last-minute notes.

Furtive, voluptuous comparisons, however, strayed through my
concentration. After all, I would be off to Cambridge in a couple
of days. There, one was catered for by a "bedder," an appellation
whose venereal-maternal overtones reinforced themselves in the fact
that some bedders were female. Oxford had no female scouts, however, and I detected, I thought, generalizing wildly on too narrow
a base, a magistral teak veneer on the scout that bedders lacked:

a minatory politeness which proved who really ran that ancient seat of learning, whatever its Hebdomadal Council thought.

My bedroom overlooked the college cemetery, an oblong trap of headstones and curbs all at conflicting angles, as if scrambled by a minor earthquake. I thought of Paul Nash's wartime painting *Totes Meer*, in which fragments of airplanes canted up from the bowels of a lugubrious marsh to recombine themselves into a Frankenstein flying machine: a Junkerschmitt 17, say, or a Focke-Dornier 109, which as the last trump sounded would bombard us all over again, this time with tons of methane-heavy magma. St. Edmund's graveyard threatened a like resurgence, its composite outcome a giant Latin-booming head on a sketchy trunk, come to repel boarders from the uncouth north. I shivered for all three days; the tiny hall stood over an icy meer, I guessed, and the little electric fire in my sitting room warmed only the peeling frame. Yet the magic of old Oxenford prevailed: one came here precisely to be cold, for cold made the mind adept. The only hot water of the day arrived in a tin jug with the scout at seven A.M. and poured from a kettle at teatime. "Gently with the gas, sir, and the power," he said, as if advising how to handle two beloved artifacts. "The *austerity*, you know." Certainly no south wind frolicked in his voice. It was 1947, year of a feral, embattling winter such as I never again saw until, a decade later, I discovered January in Montreal. The little kitchen reeked of grease, gas, and mouse dirt, but it was Cathay to me. Some of the headstones I

perused were of the fourteenth century. I had taken a train right
into history, a train that did not stop and had no terminus; no matter how many times you changed, it bore you on, then dropped
you off while other passengers went gratefully ahead.

Awed, and with chattering teeth, my mind intoning a round
based on the title *Aula Sancti Edmundi,* I ran into Vice-Principal
Kelly, a forbiddingly tall, aquiline-faced theologian, whose hand-
shake descended diagonally from a black-clad altar six feet high.
It was like shaking hands with St. Patrick himself, except that this
saturnine young cleric spoke in impetuous diphthongs about
having just played squash, of which game I had never heard, even
though I played it later on and became almost proficient. I had
never met such jovial fellows in my life, not even those who
rented out donkeys at the seaside or massacred rabbits in the
Sitwell woods, and could only conclude that these sublime luminaries—fellows indeed—who ran colleges were forever either ill-
suppressing convulsions of mirth at the awkward antics of
examinees or tuned in to some acerb transubstantial farce. One
inadvertently looked around for the master of the revels, in the
dreadful iron-clanging, earthenware-cisterned lavatories, in the
staircase tunnels that led from quad to quad (or court to court),
even in the examination room itself, where the scouts of St.
Edmund continually stoked up and fussed over a fire that had no
right to be indoors: a Dickensian conflagration that made one long
for the moment when the doors opened and someone said,

"Gentlemen, you may begin." One literally warmed to one's task as, outside in the cold, young men still in residence even during vacation coughed and joked on their way across the quad in bulky red-and-yellow scarves.

This time around, my state of mind had shifted through a degree or two of arc: the intoxication was there still, but less with the chance to show off, to kick over the Gradgrind traces, than with the opportunity to sit and write about the things that delighted me in my heart of hearts. No examination as such, this was an invitation to further enchant the converted: a swelled-headed reading of the circumstances, to be sure, but one that precluded tyro's nerves and found me, I recall, smiling complacently at the foolscap as each examination began. The Fellows of the Colleges wanted to know what I knew and could do, I told myself, and not what I didn't or couldn't. That civilized affirmativeness drew me out into a phalanx of rippling, ill-juxtaposed sentences in which I somehow conveyed my unique stance on the Sitwells, my modified astonishment at Plato's famous divided line, and, preposterous as I now find it when I think of the predominantly literary context, my nympholeptic air-mindedness, all the way from Daedalus to Sir Frank Whittle's jet engine. A youth of fragments who might not grow into a man of parts, I acquitted myself with a confidence I had been obliged to invent. And then, along with several other candidates, I entrained for Cambridge, an old hand on that battlefield, I reckoned, vaingloriously reassuring myself that, if all else failed, I was the only one of them who had played cricket for his county's Boys. Surely Derbyshire sporting prowess would win the day should the lowdown on the Sitwells fall. I dashed a few lines home on letterhead I was not entitled to, in an envelope enhanced with St. Edmund's arms.

Weird as it felt, I was beginning to know my way around colleges. Such familiarity would never be allowed to go to waste. Again porridge, beans and bacon, marmalade and cupric-tasting tea began our day. Burned, flour-costive soup and vile beef curry, followed by jam tart, were the lunch. Pipsqueak ironists, we protested our conviction that England had *won* the war, not lost it, so why the frontline rations? One boy produced a cherrywood pipe and lit it, biliously intense. We all dashed out for postcards and little handbooks to the colleges. A London candidate actually purchased the college's tie, which our Oxford contingent thought a bit thick, though just as sure of ourselves as he. We invested shillings in gifts at one remove, those of the tourist rather than the rightful occupant: mugs ablaze with shields and unglossed Latin, calendars of punts on the river and daffodils on the Backs, frangible spoons with runcible lozenges of heraldry soldered in misalignment to their tops.

It rained each day. There were, of course, no daffodils. We poled no punts. The college was eerily still, a bell jar for wood smoke and the reek of boiling greens. I bought a big map of Cambridge and eyed the jet-black plan view thereon of Oliver

Cromwell's college, but stayed away. I felt a gathering sense of being in the midst of what the Greeks called *kairos*, seasonal time as distinct from mere chronicity. A thousand perceptions added up to fifteen sentences an hour, penned oblivious of clock or question. I wrote what I had come there to write, engraving the tablets before me with a horrendous mixture of gossip, purloined epigrams (just one of my own, which began, "The annals of anguish belie themselves"), and quotations learned by heart and fist and squeezed through the cheesecloth of critics whose true vocation, I later saw, should have been horology.

"Who," T. R. Henn, the Yeats expert, asked me at my interview, "was Tully?" I babbled parabolical guesswork, slouching towards Cambridge to be born. Tully—was—*Cicero*! Had I *read* any Cicero? With blinking frustration I had, puzzled by a vehicle that so much competed with its tenor; had not Cicero's head and right hand been put on public view by Antonius? But this was sailing too near the wind; I reverted to my Yeatsian *moutons*, then dodged sideways into Edith Sitwell's *Gold Coast Customs*, a Byzantium of the aorta.... The kind and keen man cleared his throat but let me flow, and what happened after that I scarcely remember. A paralyzing ecstasy set in. St. Edmund's had telephoned St. Catherine's, as if through some interdenominational holy line. I had to choose, Henn said: if Cambridge, it would have to be Selwyn College, because it was Selwyn's turn (some such rigmarole). To ecclesiastical, red-brick Selwyn I walked, choked with mystery, but in the end chose St. Edmund, perhaps because of that ancient graveyard, or lofty Kelly in his dog collar, or those vast fires they built you to write by.

The impossible had happened. Then the possible erupted. There would be a mandatory two-year delay. While I did my military service, returning veterans would complete their interrupted studies, and then I could take up my scholarship. There was no way round it; the rule held at both places, and, it was suggested, a couple of years in uniform made a boy into a man as well as into a maturer student. But, having tasted ambrosia, I wanted a steady diet of it; I wanted to become not a man but a student, and an immature one at that. So I made what was then a sickening decision, almost as bad as going military: I settled for a provincial university, on an award I never even competed for but which came like a free sample in the mail after I passed a routine exam. Not quite my own executioner, but feeling every inch my own pawnbroker, I one day took the train to Birmingham, and three years later kept my appointment with Oxford, not in St. Edmund's *aula* after all, but in the college, Lincoln, that unleashed John Wesley on the pagan world. Anticlimax it surely was, yet one loaded with procrastinated joys. It began one of the happiest times of my life, perhaps because, once installed, I did next to no work at all, having done it, as it were, before arrival, during a succession of radiant summers whose uninsistent fleecy clouds partnered in my mind the blackened margins of innumerable books and print that swam and jigged until I knew not page from sky. I had flown blind through books, had learned the clouds by heart, confusing knowledge with magic, as always. Not facts but the fingerprints on them were my obsession; or, indeed, the etching of the whole palm: whorls, forks, asterisks, semiquavers, and scalpel-sharp crescent moons; or even, after overzealous chiromancers of the eighteenth century, the signatures or planets of our feet, which, facing earth, receive the weakest light and dwell, according to one Fludd, in a microcosmic night. An additional source of delight was that I remained still unclaimed by the military; what on earth, I wondered, would I have been useful for in Korea?

How stably you go home again, in your mind's eye unerringly plant a love tap at first base. The aerie room in which I studied looks out still at a golf course where, during winter floods, Gerald White, my grandfather's major domo, drowned while saving a sheep. My school books are there, like empty oxygen cylinders, dusted off by my mother the same day each week, in case I ever need them again, need to start over. No, that room is a bit of a shrine for a mostly absent son. The gilt on the spine of the *Short History of English Literature* has wanned beyond bleach into invisibility; the cover of my pocket selection of French verse from Ronsard to Valéry has given its friendly cobalt-blue back to the pouring afternoon sun; Russell's *Problems* falls apart if moved, into tiles of pages dangling from glue-faceted threads that set the teeth on edge; the dampwarped *Boy's Own Astronomy Handbook* still tells the truth, sidereally reliable although written before the Hiroshima bomb. I can still, thank goodness, lean my elbows on the sticky-topped table and peer again at the black-and-white photograph of the globular cluster M 13 in Hercules, scintillating eight inches and twenty-two thousand light years from my retinas. M 13's electric bull's-eye of spattered light, a boy's rune, awes again, anachronistically crinkling like silver paper in a match's flame. Yet it has a humdrum counterpart on our own planet: not the photograph in my old album, but one of those miraculous patterns traced by programmed worms. Fuzzy as the state of mind in which I competed for my sweet tomorrow, this pattern's winning caption says, after a number: cloud path generated by a gentle worm.

2

"Up"

SIXPENCE

My Oxford supervisor, John Sparrow, Fellow of All Souls College, would always escort me downstairs from his rooms and usher me to the gate, where he stood watching me out of sight as I strolled up the High Street toward Lincoln, my own college. This gesture or stance of his impressed me no end as a badge of Oxford's gentility: none of your rough-and-ready bonhomie from the outside world, but a cloistered amenity that did not really want to part with you and so watched you dwindle away after a lively conversation. Given the run of his books, certainly when he was away, I discovered his collection of Pater's manuscripts, the poetry of Rilke, which he much admired, and his passion for epitaphs. I was his only student, worth to him after taxes only sixpence per term, and he told me something I hardly believed at the time, but which has come home to roost in subsequent years. At Oxford, whatever else you think you are doing, you are unwittingly absorbing something unique and choice—a sense of the unfailing caliber of mental things, providing you with indestructible inner resources in after-years. He was right. Oxford had, still has, a kind of permanent Zeitgeist, indefinable but unmistakable.

It was against this inward pastoral (whatever it was) that you sited the slow-mo antics of port-sodden dons, the smart-alec chit-chat of well-to-do youths, and the arrival from America of such as George Steiner, who, entering Balliol, waved at the college porter and asked for cablegrams to be brought at once to his room. He waved with his deformed arm, clearly a person of enormous clout and confidence. At least as he saw it. Myth surrounded him from the first, telling us he had graduated from the University of Chicago at fifteen, or was it fourteen, and had actually spent time at Princeton in the very institute that housed Einstein. Clearly he was going to make lethal inroads on bucolic Oxford, whose dreaming spires were not going to be up to his streaming desires. Balliol, that foreign loch of invincible Scotsmen, was just the place for him. Steiner ended up writing some rather fey poetry for his pamphlet in a series I too figured in, along with other poets, two or three of them Americans. Steiner's rosy cheeks, as of a Hasidic cherub, suggested someone of preternatural health with an excellent blood supply, but his withered arm gave the lie to that, though you were not obliged to accept his yarn that he had contracted the deformity in an Algerian brothel. Actually, Steiner reminded me of a figure from a horror movie of my childhood: a crouched, obtuse personage whose rigid, defective arm stuck out in front of him and waggled about, both a warning and an entreaty.

In many ways Oxford was cosmopolitan, both college and university swarming with foreigners, North Americans and South Africans especially, loud with quaint homespun accents and expensive-looking clothes, the Americans neat but sometimes flashy, the South Africans toned down so as not to offend, drabness verging on what we called subfusc, a draper's darkness invented on the veldt. Housed in Southfield House, Lincoln College's annex for graduate students, I soon got into the swim: we were all outsiders, some of us from Cyprus and Egypt, others from Australia, Wales, Scotland, with just a sprinkling of Anglos for good measure. The college was famous for having hot and cold running water in every room, thanks to an opportunistic ploy by the Rector, Keith Murray, who during the war had leased the college to the Royal Air Force, who had promptly fitted parts of it out. Was this why he still wore his blue-gray RAF greatcoat (thick luxurious Crombie minus its epaulet stripes of course) when whisking from one quad to another on his daily inspections of the college. In a sense, he was still in the RAF, in the Reserve, and wanted to show the flag in no matter how subdued a way.

Eminent for many things, but notorious for its food, Lincoln drove us to seek lunch at other colleges, most of all Christchurch, whose gourmet fare I sampled as the guest of American poet Donald Hall, famed denizen of Harry's New York Bar in Paris. No women in Southfield House in those days, and in the hall there was a book in which to declare our goings and comings. We were supposed to be back by ten in the evening, but ground-floor windows were always open, and Mrs. Cassell and her drear husband were none too punctilious about "keeping the book."

There really wasn't much to do. Lectures were there if you wanted them, although some of us were obliged to attend Dr. Beck's nine A.M. Merton spiels on Locke, Berkeley, and Hume, to fill a degree requirement. You saw your tutor or supervisor, and got on with it, plus an occasional trip to the Bodleian Library where, to begin with, on receiving your green admission card, you had to swear you would not set fire to the place or do other disgusting things therein. You "read" for your degree, as Oxford puts it, the implication being that all the wisdom was already between covers if only you were lucky enough to find it. It had all been said, and here you were regurgitating it for those who had long ago written it all down. I must say the phrase "read for a degree" had a curiously snobby overtone, as if to imply that all the labor done at other universities (except Cambridge and Trinity College, Dublin, with whom Oxford has a quasi-Masonic deal) was a waste of time. You read, you sometimes listened, and you sometimes wrote a weekly essay. It was all very gentlemanly and sedate. The women worked much harder than the men, but often fared worse in the final result, a fact much discussed in the Oxford of today (classes of women only, in the age of coeducation and cohabitation, may be the answer).

SUGAR

In no time at all, rubbing shoulders with the best and the brightest from all over the world, you became worldly, learning that you were here to talk and talk. The tutors who taught you were your fellow students. What a good-natured zoo it was. "You talk differently," my mother said. "It hasn't taken *you* long to acquire that accent." Only eight weeks in fact. "Are you getting snobby?" "Heaven forbid," I told her. I was revamping my speech under the guidance of Lynn Bartlett, Geoffrey Bush, Donald Hall, Glen Maddy, Bud Stanton, and John Walsh; Lindsay Cousins and Max Grimmett; Hans Berker, Tony Fleischer, and Derek Philcox, even if, in my zeal to now and then talk with an American accent (a hopeless quest), I managed only to get off such enriching ballast as *yeah*s, *okay*s, and *sure*s, quite failing in my endeavors to say the stressed "it" one heard so much about, as distinct from the scanted, minor "it" of local usage: "If you would like this album for your own collection," says the Voice of America, "you can pur-chase *it* by...." Why the emphasis, I wonder; as if we might have forgotten what the sentence was about and the speaker didn't want sotto voce "it" to vanish into the semantic twilight before the bargain concluded. I could never balance my utterances so as to insert this unnecessary stress late on, and I detected a fundamental lack of faith in the efficacy of pronouns in purveyors of "*it.*" The high-wind reminder is how I thought of it, a singling out of something from the flock of itself. And I stuck to the local convenient custom, an "it" meek as a sandwich.

After a term or two, I came to realize that the Americans, some of them by now my friends, while possessing what struck me as "normal" names (John Walsh, Bernard Stanton, Lynn Bartlett, say), often referred to names quite different from their own: names uncouth and visceral-sounding, as of creatures from another planet, but exciting for their raw immediacy—Laird Cregar, Knute Rockne, Clu Gulager, Yogi Berra, which I at once related to the few I already knew, such as Zane Grey. I even fantasized such Americanized names as Mel Glerg, Stu Brarz, Blew Berry, belatedly working my way with the help of time and chronic Americana to such as Sweetbreads Bailey, Lou Tost, Chico Salmon, Cookie Lavagetto, Goody Rosen, Darryl Strawberry, Newt Minnow, Birdie Tebbetts, Stepin Fetchit, and Birch Bayh. Or Toots Mondello, Frank Froeba, George van Eps, Hymie Schertzer, Nick Fatool. This was a dimension denied most locals, whose tendency to nicknaming had a decorous element. The answer, I surmised, came from the onomatopoetic barrage of other languages that had invaded America, easing taboos and proprieties, and indeed truncations and abbreviations invented by impatient immigration inspectors on Ellis

Island. Somehow, the wilder a name became, the more the owner blossomed, drawn by the nose into a maelstrom of vocables afflicted by the New World passion for cutting things short (though contrarily retaining automobile for car). In this circus of phonemes, ripe slang dangled alongside outrageous truncation. Who would ever learn how to do it who had not been born to it? Yet between this mish-mash or tsimis and American literature, I sensed there was only the narrowest gulf.

We argued over meals, at lectures on Politeness in *The Iliad*, on the red bus from Oxford to Cowley (where Southfield House was, next to the college cricket field), and privately with clever girls. And of course we had one another to tea, an indispensable Oxford ritual, except that if you went to tea at a women's college the door had to remain open throughout (still, a better option than the older rule requiring the bed to be shoved out into the hallway). Oxford has come a long way since then.

Each of us in Southfield House had a huge bedsitter, none of that old business of the "scout" who made your bed for you and brought hot water, firewood. Mrs. Cassell made the bed and regaled us each day with Wild West Country tales in her gentle burr of a brogue. We were being mothered in the mildest way, and she got a giggle from the whole deal. I eyed and hoped to memorize what William James called the big buzzing blooming confusion of people picking their bliss and going after it unimpeded: Tony Fleischer, whose facial skin looked worn and paper-thin after some incinerative ordeal, on the Oxford-Cowley bus getting arrested for biting an attractive girl's ear. I had been reading André Gide on the *acte gratuit*, and Tony seemed to fit the bill, admiring and then acting. Not long after, I knocked at his door for some trivial reason and entered to find Tony in a lather, erect, and on a narrow table an old girl friend of mine, Olga from St. Hugh's, reading French, supine under a long towel, perspiring freely. Clearly this was a diptych I wasn't needed at, so I left them to it, sensing that Olga was already a goner. Indeed, she had been a goner before she became a goner. Tony, who had some aspiration to becoming a novelist and readily spoke of such phenomena as the veil of blood "seen" behind closed lids on a sunny day, had his earthy side too, often telling hectic stories in Anglo-Afrikaans, from which I gleaned a single Bantu word (*simba* for lion) without realizing the source, then, of his derogatory word *kaffir* (from the Arabic for infidel and, as my dictionary says, "*often not cap. chiefly SoAfr: usu disparaging: any black African*"). His interests, bordering on anthropology, struck me as being in psychology. It was he who told tales of his acquaintance with Princess Margaret and, later, with the film actress Dagmar Wynter, whose name eventually became Dana. Tony seemed well-connected, and full of the life force, whereas Hans Berker, from Windhoek, was on a different tack altogether, especially interested in Albert Schweitzer of Lambaréné, winner in 1952 of the Nobel Peace Prize, but a unique interpreter and editor of Bach, whose book *J. S. Bach: The*

Musician-Poet Hans kept by him, more entranced by the career of the historical Schweitzer than that of the historical Jesus. Perhaps what haunted him was the keyboard image of the good man finding in Bach the best expression of a righteous soul. If so, Hans, who had only a year to go when I arrived, had found in Oxford the right place: it was all organs.

Features toughened by misfortune and pain, Wilfrid Sheed had been crippled by polio and condemned to walking with sticks. He gallantly developed a yen for cricket and became a proficient scorekeeper at Lincoln's cricket matches. We gathered he was the son from the Sheed and Ward publishing family and would go on to edit *Commonweal* and *Jubilee*, as well as compose books of mordant prose. Ernest Hofer was not only seeking an Oxford degree, he was commuting to Paris to get an extra one, prelude to a career in academe, which he in fact took up.

All going their own way, David Yardley toward a chair in law and a fellowship at St. Edmund Hall, Derek Flower to (presumably) a career as a pianist (he played the baby grand in his room all the time), the whole gang of us on one occasion staging in my room a cross-dressing cocktail party with much use of satin wraps and coral lipstick. Yardley, we and the invited nurses decided, was the best-looking dame, a true blonde with fresh, Irish skin. Mostly we drank South African sherry, cheap and fruity, unable to lash out for gin or scotch. Oxford had as many nurses as Corregidor and they were always game for a party, no-nonsense earthy women who kept us in sugar and butter (this was the tail-end of wartime rationing, so when you "went up to Oxford," you were obliged to take your ration book with you). When, a couple of years later, I sailed to New York to visit Columbia, I still had to take it with me, only to abandon it in America as useless. Perhaps the nurses, tending to our sweet tooth and lust for fat, thought we would become a good catch; I doubt it—they sensed a good time in the offing and freely handed out what Oxford girls (with some exceptions) kept to themselves. One of my stricter Oxford girls berated me for loafing around like a cat, looking and looking, little realizing that in those days I was an observant wannabe, lasciviously malingering.

MAPS OF THE TRENCHES

Anyone composing such a view as this is bound to have lost touch with some individuals vividly remembered: Bernard Dawson of Sheffield, suave and malleable, born in the same part of England as I was, and close to the family of the poet Cecil Day Lewis; Christopher Ruscombe-King, who vanished suddenly for reasons never known, and Roger Michaelides of Cyprus who headed back to his native island for some destination in politics; Owen Harries, busy reading Orwell and snappily disputing the caliber of other authors, but compulsively well-read; Tommy Hardie, economist, about whom I remember only the story he told about himself, having pleasured some nurse, only to wake up with his penis glued to the sheet. Perhaps for him a future in superconductors. One never knows. And then Glenn Maddy and Bernard (Bud) Stanton, the latter of whom I remet in Ithaca after long years, he looking rather military, I thought. I had never had so many friends, both in college and out. John Walsh had taught me how to read *Time* magazine. Lynn Bartlett, heading back to Vassar to become a dean, counseled me on writing to chairpersons about a job—the American way of applying, so far from the circumlocutions of the local one.

Of course, such things as *The Lincoln College Record* keep you abreast of college affairs and people, not least through the obituary columns. *Oxford Today*, "The University Magazine," seems to concern itself mostly with faculty and Oxford poets (as distinct from novelists). Prose, virtuosity in which gets you in, or got, seems to have lost ground or face in contemporary Oxford, as if it were vulgar. I had a deep misgiving when the *Lincoln Record* announced it would henceforth go on-line, meaning it would arrive as a floppy disc. Alas, being a Luddite, I have no place to insert a floppy disc, so I would never know who had died or published. Happily, however, a new issue has just arrived, a readable one, so perhaps protesting Luddites have prevailed and the college has gone back to its old ways of chummy or acidulous write-up: prose on the page and no machine in between. Not long ago the college announced the compilation of a Who's Who and asked for biographical details. I sent mine, but apparently not enough old members did, and the project died unborn, a pity in a way because it would have made old friends easier to find. People sometimes want to be left alone, which I respect, never having been one for college gaudies, though a distant and critical observer of the cricket scores.

I am looking at all this, this "new life," as through the one eye of my soldier father, leaning against his cherished place at the bar in the local pub, a Duke of York, his face clean-shaven for this nightly occasion, his Croix de Guerre insignia neatly dusted off with a flick of his little finger, his pipe lit and coming gradually to the seethe (slight dottle of spit in the bottom of the bowl).

"How's *your* boy, then?"

"Playing quite a bit of cricket. He's at Oxford, you know." He might just as well have said the Moon or Timbuktu. All mighty inaccessible, certainly from that niche against the bar. I was his torpedo, perhaps his last one, not that he had made any attempt to launch me; but he was glad of any damage I did, seeing, as he did, all upward striving as a continuation of the First World War. He had enlisted at sixteen, faking his age; blown up by a shell three years later, blinded, then only half-blind.

Then he would tell them what I had said in my most recent letter, ignoring the intellectual parts because history was what interested him most. It was something to do with his colossal memory, apart from sticking pin-flags into maps of the trenches.

"Studying hard, I bet?"

"Nothing that would break his spirit." My father reserved an almost liturgical-surgical serenity for these occasions.

"But working hard all the same," the knowing voice, of almost anyone among the companionable drinkers, insisted.

"It makes Jack a dull boy," my father replied. "Anyway, they don't go *there* just to *work*. It isn't that kind of place, like the Army, the Navy, the Marines, oh no. They go *there* to *meet* one another, then they come home to read. But I suppose you have to *live with* it to understand the finer points, if you take my meaning. It's no good guessing about it from the outside. Take the Boat Race. From outside, you'd have no idea what they go through, just to get into it, and how much they have to give up just to get picked, see. You can't just waltz off into a punt or a skiff and row down the Thames. Or is it up? You need to be *within*."

"Oh, will he be rowing then?"

"No, he doesn't like water. He'll be on the bank, cheering. It's not exactly a football match."

"Oh, we can see that," they tell him. "It's all very mysterious and posh, isn't it?" My father sucks on his dark blue pipe, Thamesside already.

Sometimes the memoirist or memorialist, whether excavating misery or joy, is much like the brain surgeon who drills holes in the brainpan, then leaves them alone until he has finished, plugging them for the time being with sterile beeswax. One digs or bores around, even if only to prepare a retreat from the scene of action. And then, of course, the service holes begin to yield up disbanded memories, and the excavator, punctilious to the point of fatuity, cannot leave them alone. Why should he or she? Proust speaks delicately, though with some condescension, of the voluntary memory, but it's the involuntary one he really cares about—what I call the inadvertent memory, which I think we sometimes scant because we think it's familiar whereas it's not. To put it another, less cranial way, I sometimes feel unrequited by sunlight, I who winter in the subtropics and there find my energy doubled. It is as if the sun, offering so much in its blindingly constant way, does not offer enough, as if its all were inadequate. One always wants more. So too with memory, especially when we fail to recognize what, say, has come to the surface about Oxford. Perhaps one even tires of the coming-to-the-light quality of the things that do, unaware that they are nonpareils.

Well, my heroic father whose effective life virtually ended in his teens after prodigious feats in the Flanders mud, would sometimes pore over his maps with an unusual expression hard to define; but you could see he was wishing hard, for something to have happened, or not to have, and he was taunted by the mystery of what he used to think of as inevitability. A big oval wound scar on his back reappeared on mine, still there, and we knew this could not be true. Perhaps such an expression of facial confoundment would like to deny the matrix from which what happens comes. It would like nothing to have happened at all, content to be left with a blank. He wanted very much to unremember. I, years after Oxford, felt bothered by the sheer modernity of my response, to my having more or less overlooked the ancientness of the place, its flow from the Middle Ages onward. I was among ghosts, old stones, hallowed sites available to everyone, and I had missed them until I went back, astounded to find how close the university had been to the church, to an Old Testament full of threats. Hand in glove amid the burnings. When John Sparrow was elected Warden of All Souls, he explained that he, as pagan as I, would go through the motions required at the altar, and that was that. I was amazed.

I should not have been. Now I looked around me at all the colleges devoted to Christianity. The Visitor to my own college was the Bishop of Lincoln. Where could such as he feel more at home than among Jesus College, Christchurch, Corpus Christi College, Magdalen College, St. Hilda's, St. Hugh's, St. Anne's Society? There were secular foundations, to be sure, but what could a Jew or Hindu do in such a place, not to mention all the African tribal leaders who passed through before going home to assegai and shield, or, indeed, my supervisor, formerly a legal aide-de-camp in Washington with a first in ancient history and literature (Latin and Greek)? Adaptable, for perhaps political reasons, he was papering over the paper that already papered over the cracks, and, when he showed me the bare bedchamber he had been assigned to, I thought it resembled a monk's cell, austere and stark. Now the tremendous hold of the church on English politics became clear, as indeed of English versus Roman. I ended up writing a short story set in the Middle Ages, spoken by the abbot of an ancient college, pondering the bleakness of his religious-donnish life. Lincoln's main kitchen was built in the early fifteenth century and sometimes smelled like it.

Set aside for a moment my presence on a favorite destination of Lincoln's bishop, no matter how worthy a soul he be, and consider my visits to the college of All Souls, which sounds a bit like overdoing it. *All* souls, including heathen ones? I wondered what was going on in the image's comprehensive clutch, which surely implicated the managerial activities of my gay accomplice the warden. Trying to grapple with the facile-seeming totality of the college's name (no humbler than the more materialistic *All Things Considered* of National Public Radio in a later age), I wondered further if somehow all the souls there were poured into the college's upstairs dimension in an ever-narrowing stream rather like those downward-pointed clouds that enclose the words of speakers in comics. Or was the "allness" taken for granted from the start? Without a single shift on any soul's part, the soul belonged here anyway from the very beginning. If so, who was the mighty possessor, the unthinkably vast celebrant who looked after everybody's spiritual welfare? To enter so theological a city as Oxford with such misgivings is unwise, of course; you at once run into all kinds of casuistry, taken mostly in one's stride as a quaint leftover from seven hundred years earlier. What if it were *All Minds*, or *All Intellects*? Wouldn't that be more contemporary, more in tune with modern suppositions? Well, the only way to get over it was to regard it as auld poesie, with cynicism saved up for later when your link to these institutions was less firm.

I never could, though, usually schooling myself to think of the university as a grocery handed over to God, who owned all souls anyway. What the colleges did not need was some upstart youngster determined to make sense of time-honored allusions or junk them as so much window-dressing fol-de-rol. Were other universities that religious, even in the aftertaste? I thought not, excepting only Cambridge and possibly Trinity College, Dublin, the two other members of the holy trio. Yet Cambridge had its own divine-flavored places such as Trinity, Jesus, and Magdalene, and the Dublin variant had its own Trinity to begin with. Could the explanation be merely that this was a holy, tradition-worshipping country and the religious taint (as I saw it) was something to be assimilated along with the eroticism of Spenser's poetry, Tennyson's rather haughty nature lyricism ("Come into the garden, Maud"), and Milton's superb cosmic paraphernalia? I wondered how much the university's ancient imagery would get in the way of logical or opportunistic thinking. What on earth did scientists make of this heavy dollop of piety, hanging on like those limbs in anatomy that, although rotten, have not fallen off and are called marcescent? Warden Sparrow would officiate at the altar much as he had in uniform in Washington, D.C. Clearly, one's sense of role-playing would have to improve, and not be so literal.

For all I cared, the colleges could have been affiliated with Firestone, Boeing, or Rolls-Royce. I was hunting the cachet, I suppose, the name-brand, and quite wisely too. Now, however, safely within the perimeter on a research fellowship, I was beginning to carp. I realize that, if my approach had been more historical, it would have been less pagan. The image in my mind of the seedy, forlorn head of a religious college brooding on things in the Middle Ages was closer to the mark. His hands were tied by what he worked in, and his mind was not obligated, as I think mine was, to that wholly new imagery of airplanes, atom bombs and LSD, out of which I eventually grew. My American friends, who might well have cavilled, took the matter with wry aplomb, and I learned from them to sail through. I was being solemn.

NOURISHERS

Picture then the young inquisitor freed at last from theological worries, beginning to enjoy life by writing for *Isis*, attending *Isis* parties, reading a paper to this or that college society, dining at the Union, actually getting to work in the Bodleian, and of course playing cricket, after which, often enough, we repaired to Lincoln's Deep Hall ("Harry Deepers") for beer. I began going to movies, encouraged in this by the Canadian movie-maker Paul Almond, and sometimes to concerts, my love of classical music having traveled with me unscathed. In between times, even the least adventurous of us trafficked with the two bosomy Welsh sisters whose ambition, so it was said, had long been to sleep with the entire college, though the math might have become a problem. And there was always Melanie Chegbrogan, handmaiden of the handgallop for emergencies, marred only by her mustache, which may or may not enter into the arrangement. She, and other nurses, would arrive with groceries snatched from the eager mouths of patients, thus calling the food to a higher service, maybe, I mused, the higher service of Jesus himself. You never knew. Most Oxford women worked too hard and must have joined chastity with industry to store up credit in heaven.

It was said, by youths whose sisters visited the college on a regular basis, no doubt to earn their quota, that the really serious nurses, who had been on the wards at night for many a year, ministering and soothing, would arrive with the usual contraband of sugar and butter, plus possibly jam and cheese or eggs, but also a fresh pack of rubber gloves, whose very appearance from the basket became proof of the pudding. Then you knew you were in for it: defilement by rubber, and no holds barred. Clearly these experienced ladies had a much better chance of prevailing over an entire college's several hundred souls than two Welsh sisters, whose clandestine antics in Southfield House had led to at least two nightly crashes of the broken bed. They were putting too much heart into their labors, I thought, having been next door to one such detonation of bliss, and do the sisters cheat on the addition? How can they possibly keep it straight? Does a busted bed count double? Our lofty intellectual ardor needed an outlet of some kind, although not at the hands (or lips) of Stefanie Blythe, whom I once encountered at a dance (I did not dance but shuffled around the floor as if spastic) and chatted up until I discovered she was a lip and tongue biter who drew blood but nothing else. I wonder who's kissing her now.

The more understanding nurses also kept the sweet-toothed among us in our favorite sweetmeats: *Aero* chocolate, honeycombed with holes and therefore light; *Kit-Kat*s, which were four fingers of biscuit encased in milkier chocolate, and such other dental wreckers as mint imperials, chocolate logs, licorice, *Mars* and *Milky Way* bars, Jelly Babies, Pontefract Cakes (slimy black penny-like things), *Nipits*, and Spanish Juice. Not many of us smoked, hence the craving for things sweet. You could just about tell what someone had been masticating from his breath— minty, oily, milky, or the sweet bleak bark-like aroma of licorice. It was always a startling confrontation, this: the high-powered brain dispensing aphorisms lifted from Wittgenstein (who seems to have invented up in Manchester a propeller-tip jet engine) next to an almost nursery bouquet of creamy chocolate, as if we had never grown up. Someone drawing attention to the way Henry James interrupts his characters or Matthew Arnold italicizes his favored words would also be giving you a Cadbury boost of maltreated cocoa. Or we chewed bubblegum throughout chatter on "polishing music" (fast flighty tempo for brasses) or the way some people, when being introduced, encapsulate themselves in one salient word said mildly: *humdrum* or "a simple country boy."

One early reader of these early pages actually suggested that an Oxford life such as this was "rarefied," whereas *I* thought it was at least reified, and even down to earth or profane. Such an observation provided a hint, I supposed, of the gibberingly bestial depths one American woman expected of us, and had at least hoped for. Having been rarefied, I felt rather pleased that during our most primal rites with nourishers and others we were still the hard-core intellectuals our sponsors and parents hoped we were. One could only guess at the chronic depravities of Harvard and Yale three thousand miles away where carnal knowledge was truly infernal. Imagination opens many raincoats, and leaves them gaping.

3

Sez

POBBLE

More research than you might imagine has treated the subject of Oxford speech. There is, of course, an Oxford accent which, tested against the so-called "received pronunciation" (RP) of BBC English, tops a wide gallery including the Yorkshire accent made famous by Wilfred Pickles, almost a wild beast of the moors whom the BBC had let loose to read the news in an unapologetic, broad accent that made half the nation wince, the other half leap into the streets rudely cheering. But we soon got used to him, able at times to muster an oblivion worthy of the newborn, at least as far as accent went. Lincoln College, much under Empire influence and headed by Keith Murray of Oxford *and Cornell* and Edinburgh, evolved an almost pragmatic mode of speech quite without distinctive fanciness, perhaps the kind of English preferred by the Royal Air Force when I got into the business of officer training (and accent vetting). Indeed, the RAF had declared its preference for the more lucid kind of Scots accent, excluding the opaque mutters of football managers.

One of our local sports was to walk down High Street (the High) on the All Souls side to the whereabouts of a certain café, outside which a little clique of fruity-toots assembled daily to air their diphthongs to passers-by. Now their spoken English was an oral marvel, full of elaborate looping twirls, carefully nurtured vowels, far too many "extrOrdinary"s and "*e*ctuelly"s, but imitable as we found. They fluted away on the café side of the High while we parodied them opposite. Of course, it takes years of practice to mangle English in their fashion, starting in the nursery maybe, but one can manage it roughly, first of all learning to produce whooping, leaping vowels that change English into a monster of enormous vertical range. You need more "I says"s and "I deeownt suppose"s, but most of all you have to approach speech as if it were oratorio, with everyday conversation almost sung. Hand gestures follow, but the emphasis is on the phoneme: meaningful units of minimal sound-speech, a definition I'd had rammed into me when I was seventeen. At least I now knew what I was talking about. I have never been able to develop those rhapsodical roller-coasters of public-school utterance, those languid laissez-faire drawls of the comfortably off, those toots and warbles and hyperbolic vocal curtseys. Had I been at Cambridge I would have found it easy to achieve what one heard so often there: the Cambridge lisp, the Cambwidge lithp as pwactithed by so distinguished an exponent as Jacob Bronowski who, it is worth noting, spent part of his career among bluff Yorkshire folk at the University of Hull.

All this mangling of some Platonic form of English struck us, the no-nonsense highbrows of Lincoln, as pure affectation, in other words nothing but affectation. Was it worth acquiring, to humble the lower classes with or to shock our parents, to amaze interviewers with and so gain a better job? We didn't think so, but some of us ended up with South African or American intonations or even an Aussie "gdye." Of course, in the devout background there were the English Department's Tolkien, professor of Anglo-Saxon and eventual deviser of Hobbits, and other dons all talking some polyglot language far from the supposed Oxford norm. Posher colleges had more exponents of refined, upper-class English, I suppose, whereas the rougher colleges—Nuffield, Ruskin, St. Anthony's, St. Catherine's Society—dealt in a hodge-podge of the unfashionable. I came out speaking what non-Oxford people think of as Oxford English: a poor thing but mine own, an aural album of contingency samples from hither and yon, some of it Oxford tootle, I suppose, but not half so exaggerated a tootle as the one that comes out of New Delhi, where English literature is taught (to judge by my own students from there) in the most authentically Oxford accent imaginable. Lumped together, New Delhi and I talk funny—and don't intend to change. If I'd never gone to Oxford I might have spoken village English forever: uncouth, mumbled, close to Old Norse.

I have remembered Bronowski's lisp but almost forgotten Isaiah Berlin, who "pobbled." To pobble is to gobble suavely, a trick invented in certain public schools, its aim being to convince hearers that you are responding brilliantly to what they said, but with the entire burden of what you say lost in the polyphonic rumble of your speech. How did pobbling sound? Hard to express it in words, but something like "hob-bon bobble, wob wob, bob-bob-bob, terminally finite," the last two words thrown in to sustain the illusion of something astute just missed, thanks to the brutish sound effects. Invited to dinner at All Souls, where Berlin was a Fellow, I would put on my black tie and go sit among Oxford's worthies, all of whom spoke with lucid constraint. Only Berlin pobbled, all the way through the meal, hardly ever pausing to ingest, and answering or propounding with voluminous pobble. No one ever understood what he was saying. They waited for his books. It was hard to connect *The Hedgehog and the Fox* with this fellow, but you had to do it. He had gone to St. Paul's School in Chiswick, London, not a place for pobble, so I presume he had taught himself how to do it in front of a mirror perhaps, thus inventing the perfect way of keeping your best ideas to yourself until publication while gaining the repute of a brilliant mind on the prowl. He responded copiously to questions of my own, so perhaps I was meant to learn the pobble from him. It was amazing to sit alongside him (or Stuart Hampshire the philosopher or Lord David Cecil the literary critic) and watch everyone attentively understanding what he said, or seeming to, then using the springboard of his bottom-of-the-mouth speech to make points of their own. I later discovered that Berlin referred to his wife as Isaiahline, surely a case of pobble deriving from itself. During the war, he too in Sparrow's

Washington, he sent many erudite, witty cables to London (a unique chance of hearing him unpobbled), and after the war Winston Churchill asked America to send this Berlin to see him. They did, but they sent Irving. So Churchill, who would no doubt have appreciated his battered elocution, probably never heard pobbling at all unless he had heard it in school. Pobble, like Navajo, might have served as a wartime code, except that it had a real audience of only one.

"Dead"

At Oxford, you are always surrounded by Latin and some Greek. In the old days, which this memoir records, you had to pass an examination in Latin (or Greek) to get in, but all that has gone now, and with it, I suppose, part of my delight in coming to Latin late and getting the first hundred percent on the matriculation paper, actually rendering the prose into verse in a display of wanton hubris. Never mind. Whenever I had contact with Latin at Oxford I had a sense of minor ownership, even when I confronted the phrase *in statu pupillari*, meaning an undergraduate, still in the pupa. Or, as one dictionary puts it, an intermediate usually quiescent stage of a metamorphic insect (bee, moth, or beetle). Pupa means doll. In its enlightened way, Oxford still has three eight-week terms (take that, you semesters of American overload with your tedious fifteen-weekers): Michaelmas, Hilary, and Trinity (which might nowadays be named for someone or something else). A gaudy night is a college celebration or rejoicing, and an *encaenia* day is Latinized Greek (*en-kainos* = into the new) for a feast annually celebrated on a college's founding day. Into the new year it says, all augury. A hebdomadal council meets every seventh day (that's Greek too). Lincoln College has a Rector, who rules (except our man was gay and liked the cello). Those who serve as watchdogs over students are proctors, familiarly dubbed "bullers." The renowned program in classical Greats is otherwise called *literae humaniores*: the humaner letters, the ideal training for such Prime Ministers as Harold Macmillan, although Anthony Eden read Persian. The updated parallel program of "Modern Greats," varying from PPE (Philosophy, Politics, and Economics) to PPP (Philosophy, Politics, and Psychology) was sufficient for such as Harold Wilson, but its aura lacked the huge portmanteau learning of ancient Greats.

In a sense, although Greats restricted itself to Latin and Greek (what were the *less* humane letters implied by the title?), this was the only subject worthy of a keen, capacious mind; all others were twaddle, and I do believe there has long existed a secret society of those who had excelled in Greats, which surely exempts you from being Christian. People who know that discipline know they have "been through it" and have not been found wanting. Sparrow was one such, moving easily to a first in Honour Moderations (1927), but with some toil to his viva-ed first in Greats (1929). He won, by examination, at which he was adept, a fellowship at All Souls, then chose to enter the Middle Temple and read for the jargon-encrusted bar. When war began in 1939, in a T.E. Lawrentian flash, he enlisted as a private in the Oxfordshire and Buckinghamshire Light Infantry, next commissioned in the

Coldstream Guards. It cannot be said that the British military of
the day were slow to salute intellectual prowess once they identified it. T. E. Lawrence, author also of a stencilled, duplicated
manual on the 200 Class Royal Air Force seaplane tender and a
Fellow of All Souls, stayed on virtually unrecognized in the ranks
because he wanted to, having had his day in the sun. Sparrow
ended up as an aide-de-camp to the British Military Mission in
Washington, then on the War Office's morale committee, visiting
troops in training and on the front lines in India, Persia, Italy, and
Germany. Quite a tour for a classical scholar who liked the soldiery
but not his fellow officers.

"The rough shirts of the common soldier chafed," he once said,
to which I, amazed to be having such a banal exchange with him,
responded, "No trubenized collar?"

"Which is *what*?" he asked.

"Some trick of Van Heusen's," I told him, exhausting at one
shot my knowledge of shirt collars.

"Ah," he replied inscrutably, "a diabolical liberty, as they
say." He was soon wearing a tie anyway, after they made him an
officer, and detachable collars of soft linen.

Even as a scholarship candidate, I got into the habit of examining Latin names and relishing them. St. Edmund Hall, which
restricted itself to two genial, provocative papers in English, called
itself *Aula Sancti Edmundi*. Off again into Christian myth. *Aula*
was Hall, *Edmundi* "Teddy," as it were. The scout who looked

after you, who "saw to" you, would at Cambridge have been a gyp or bedder. Oxford has quadrangles (quads) whereas Cambridge has courts. One Oxford peculiarity is that New College is never called New (like, say, Balliol or Lincoln). You go up to Oxford and London, down to elsewhere. The old thoroughfare called Grove Street used to be called Gropecunt Lane, for obvious reasons, and we preferred it like that, for Chaucerian reasons. A Cambridge gown was long and voluminous, an Oxford gown was and is a mere square of black, not long or wide, with tapes attached. If you were a scholar of some kind at Oxford you wore a Cambridge-type gown to denote your status in the eyes of the University, and if you were a graduate student you wore a special long gown that nobody bothered to buy.

You could win a closed or open scholarship depending on your brains and ancestry, or be admitted as a commoner, which meant you were a blue blood with private means but only medium brains, or had medium brains and could also somehow manage to pay your own way for three years or more. I was amazed by the variety and quantity of such awards; academically Oxford was never the closed shop it was rumored to be, though you might be turned down on grounds of etiquette or background. A recent study of student performance came up with the bizarre but understandable finding that, at London University, two working-class students with good minds had never spoken in class, afraid of seeming uncouth or inferior by virtue of the way they spoke. Would Oxford care?

I hasten to add that the class in question was a seminar of some half-dozen, maybe more, which seems the norm at non-Oxbridge universities. The matter would not have arisen at Oxford with only one, or perhaps two, meeting the tutor at the same time. More telling, to me at any rate, who became accustomed to sitting scholarship exams (proof of my own incompetence no doubt, although in the end it paid off), is the disappearance of such examinations, much tougher in some ways than final degree papers, yet much more inviting and suggestive at the same time. If you were original, you were desirable, provided you knew Latin et cetera. The poet Louis MacNeice's responses in a scholarship exam he took were legendary; he was too good to be true, and they could see his congratulatory first gleaming from years hence.

Latin reared its august head if you were too ill to take your final exams: you were given an *aegrotat* meaning "Is ill." which no doubt echoes for some the *exeat*—the ticket of leave issued to pupils at a public school, entitling them to leave the premises. No *exeat*s at Oxford, not in my time, but if you came home late and couldn't climb back into college, the bullers might get you and hand you over to the proctors for punishment. You might even be sent down or "gated," confined to college. Nowadays with girls already within, and vice versa, the matter hardly arises. One still recalls with pleasure, however, how Oscar Wilde and his friends, caught dining out at the Clarendon (obviously an offense) by a prowling proctor, greeted his summons to his college, Jesus, opposite Lincoln, with cries of "Do we *have* to report to Jesus?"

Sex arose, though, for Peter Quennell (Balliol), biographer of Byron and editor of *History Today*, who was sent down from Balliol for some sexual transgression (as was poet and critic William Empson, from Magdalene College, Cambridge, who peered shortsightedly from the front row of Winchester College prefects photographed in 1925, the young John Sparrow well to his right, behind him). Those were the old university days, older than mine, and the sending-down a benighted custom perhaps related to the garb we were supposed to wear to examinations in the Schools (where what was lectured on was examined upon). Women were supposed to wear black stockings and black shoes, as well as dark clothing beneath the gown (to make them, supposedly, less erotic to look at!). Men wore a dark suit and a white bow tie, maybe to make them look angelic. One good thing then (at least it sounded good, but was rarely invoked): an examinee by raising his arm could request a glass of ale. Or was it a pitcher? Nor am I sure if it would help. How typical of Oxford: prudery and debauchery mingled.

The atmosphere at scholarship exams was different; the mere sight of a girl disguised as a Michelin man would no doubt have unhinged us quite. The idea may have been, in Schools as distinct from colleges, to give us all the look of clergymen. We scholarship boys couldn't wear gowns anyway since we were merely applicants and postulants. It's a wonder, though, that we were not issued some special garb consecrated to sitting for schols; even choral ones.

You do not have to be especially observant, even now, to notice how many college choirs there are, many of whom sing holy hymns, and prolifically record Handel oratorios, masses, glees, "Cries of London," polyphonic motets, anthems, antiphons, consorts of viols, sonate da chiesa, early Byrd, and more. You do not have to be very observant either to notice in your copy of *Oxford Today* a flier from "Lincoln College in association with Walters & Co (Oxford) Ltd.," 10 The Turl, offering university and college regalia for sale. The mood is a bit less altruistically esthetic, I suppose, because it sells Oxford University club neckties (Hockey Occasionals, silk; Hockey Occasionals, polyester, much cheaper; the fancier clubs offer silk, but the Azembric, Gridiron, and Greyhounds run only to polyester). A quiet current of side or snootiness polluting these fabulous offers? You can also invest in sweatshirts with or without hoods, all with crest, as well as cufflinks, wraps, tie slides and key fobs (both crested). Will all these pretties humiliate them in Fargo or win the girl marooned in Dunfermline?

Overleaf, the flier peddles Lincoln College regalia plus Boater Bands and Golf Umbrellas, as well as a small selection of "Childrenswear." A discreet note, set in an oval disc, informs you that "10% of this order will be donated to College Projects." No harm in it all, I suppose. They could be selling garden gnomes instead, though when you have commerce for a neighbor you may have a CEO in your Senior Common Room. I am reminded of Warden Sparrow's verdict on All Souls during the distant Suez crisis: "A hotbed of cold feet."

Returning to matters of high seriousness, I am happy to note that Lincoln boasted an actual composer, Egon Wellesz, among its Fellows. He was a musicologist too, of palpable distinction. If you like classical music, or even settings of psalms and hymns, as one can without at all subscribing to their burden, then a choir's presence and tunes in college aren't going to upset you, but Oxford's incessant bells might. They seemed all around me when I sat pondering Pater's manuscripts in All Souls, my supervisor having taken train to Wolverhampton to watch Billy Wright, a cult of his, play football (that is, soccer) for Wolverhampton Wanderers (the team of Sparrow's home town). Thank goodness, I thought, I live in Southfield House out in Cowley, down the High and out past the Plain, off the main highway up by a cricket field. I still have the same sensitive ears.

Why was Oxford so quasi-religious, with bells banging madly to call us to this or that service? To an extent, choirs did the same thing, but inoffensively as part of the dulcet atmosphere, best heard from outside the chapel perhaps. But the bells disturbed the sleep and thought of many I knew, reminding them of a higher service than mere thought. Would not a burst of Byrd or Tallis have done just as well, less imperious and monotonous? It was akin to commercials, was it not? Could there not have been a day of reprieve on behalf of all the atheists and agnostics, Jews and Hindus, listening? Or gamelans, gongs, bull-roarers for Australians?

A veritable fanatic of Latin, my supervisor collected epitaphs, then published the result: graveyard gravy or geezer glyphs. He gave me several volumes of them, inscribed in Latin of course: "PW, *donum datum*, JS," almost an epitaph in its own right. In other respects he wasn't funereal except when at the All Souls altar, officiating as he had to as Warden, equipped now with a huge door opening on the High, and a suite called the Warden's Lodgings. Had all this gone to his head? Not in the least. He stayed the same, faithful to his declared intention of introducing me, as his only protégé, to the best that Oxford could offer in minds, food, and friendship. He dreaded, he once told me, seeing a bright young man go through all the same hoops as thousands of other bright young men, himself included, and I began to wonder what clandestine career he envisioned for me. Declining his invitation to Venice (an annual sortie), I went off to play cricket, realizing belatedly that I had no doubt committed a gaffe, in *his* eyes at least. I never got to Venice or saw his rooms in Middle Temple Lane or Pump Court (he remained a barrister throughout his limited academic career and worked for Cyril Radcliffe, the barrister who had partitioned India, at the Chancery Bar). Shuttling by train from Lincoln's Inn in London to his Fellow's rooms in All Souls, he had begun to enjoy both lives, actually making some money as Radcliffe's junior and supplementing that with his Fellowship. It was his first experience of living in London, and he delighted in the literary and social scene: a man in demand.

Those were early days, when he collected up the esteem due to him. When I showed up twenty years later, I did not need to explain to him where I was from: he had corresponded a good deal with Edith Sitwell and, until he wearied of her mannerisms (her constant rearrangement of her hands in her lap), had been a guest at Renishaw and knew all of those esthetes who came up from London (or down), paraded through Southgate and Market Street, then went back up (or down) satiated and soothed. Quaintly enough, he kept seventy-two of her early letters to him while she kept none of his replies. After he became Warden of All Souls, she began to keep his letters while he destroyed hers.

In retrospect, Sparrow the barrister who loved the battle of wits rather than the outcome and relished his sinecure at All Souls (a fellowship that, in theory, might last forever) settles down in the mind's eye as a straddler facing both ways. He scrawls across a pamphlet from the Homosexual Liberation Movement "What an obscene document," while in the full glory of the paradoxical man, almost a parody of a closeted Oxford don, takes train to the Lady Chatterley Trial (*1960: Regina v. Penguin Books Ltd.*), after which he composes a couple of essays for *Encounter* in which with unorthodox forensic relish he proves that the gamekeeper buggers the lady—a practice he condemned. Meddling thus, unable to resist the barrister in himself, or the overlap between homo- and heterosexual mores, he must have cut an outrageous and peculiar figure, but he loathed humbug, even during a time when homosexual acts were still illegal in Britain.

One London literary editor, a kind and worldly man, on seeing my supervisor's face unluckily photographed against a brick wall, which gave him a faintly convicted look, murmured, "Poor bugger." Sometimes, *I* thought, demons had him by the short hairs. Or Furies. I was there in his rooms one day when he returned from Wolverhampton in a great commotion, having torn his thumbnail in or on the train, and the outsize hangnail just had to be clipped. He was almost panicking when the porter brought scissors and nail-file, clipped the offending fragment, and escorted me out, the one occasion when my supervisor didn't accompany me down. Was this before he became Warden? I think so, or with his Warden's shotgun he would have blown the bit of horn to smithereens.

No, he was true to his vow to show me the best and win me the good will of those brains, whatever else he neglected to do. I liked football too, so we had that in common, and we both respected decadence, about which I was writing. I had wanted to write about Byron, Pater, Eliot, even Lawrence (T. E.), but the Faculty had rejected all eighteen of my eager proposals and saddled me instead with an obscure literary periodical of the 1890s, which they found quite modern enough. So there was academic tedium, on his part too. On the whole he preferred epitaphs, but when I at last finished making a mountain out of this molehill, he at least bought the run of the forgotten magazine from me in the interests of book collecting. My little portrait of *The Dome* appeared in John Hayward's *The Book Collector*, and good riddance to it. I got around to Byron ten years later, in *Byron and the Spoiler's Art*, and Pater in several essays, but not Eliot or Lawrence.

I often wondered about my relationship with Sparrow. I was surely far from what he might have expected: some glowing youth clad in premature sophistication, a pliable person whom nothing surprised, someone with at least one silver spoon in his background. No, Sparrow left things to chance, which argued in him a Gidean flexibility I rather admired. He was not intent on making a silk purse out of sow's ear, but had heeded the Latin verb *educare* and the verb it derives from, *educere*. Both can mean to lead out or bring up. Hence education. He himself had had a splendid education at his public school; he seemed to want me to have one too. There were times when I felt adopted, learnedly attended to, as when we set ourselves up to have a true tutorial, on say the novels of Forrest Reid. One had to remember that as a mere schoolboy he had published with Cambridge University Press an edition of John Donne's *Devotions Upon Emergent Occasions*, *"with a Bibliographic Note by Geoffrey Keynes, Fellow of the Royal College of Surgeons."* At just seventeen. He had penned a winning letter to Keynes, bibliographer and literary scholar, and they had met on the steps of St. Paul's, Sparrow grinning widely under his bowler hat. Fifty years after, Sparrow admitted in a lecture that "Geoffrey Keynes turned me from a book-lover into a book-collector." Alas, some will say. Many forces, impulses, and persons drew Sparrow away from what creativity was in him, even if only a creative response to the work of others. I can only say he sympathized with fumbling youth so long as the youth was bright and eager and helplessly intellectual. You did not have to be precocious. I never saw the selfish, cruel or explosive side of him that others have reported, but an abundant sly humor, yes. In some ways he was a grown-up naughty boy who had enjoyed barracks life and platoon football.

I felt much the same when one of his neatly folded All Souls pages arrived in the mail, each adorned with cursive, almost histrionic script, executed in ink instantly blotted, which gave the letters an almost transparent, washed-out look, as if he'd tried to seal or capture the mental essence of each word as he set it down. Did he mop up, so to speak, after each word? As handwriting goes, it was contrary, with the accent on the second syllable. It would often soar away sideways, upward, never down, making wobbly what should be straight, and vice versa, with capitals grandly attuned to the emotion of the moment, and not anywhere a handover from orthodox writing lessons. It was all original, the hand of a consummately clever man, who always signed himself John. Several times I tried to mimic his swooping writing style, but gave up; I was a sumo wrestler aping Houdini, whereas

I managed now and then a fair copy of Walter Pater's less theatrical hand. Sparrow the penman had style, although in his actual writings he settled for a prose style nearly austere, as if treading on stepping stones through No Man's Land. What was the jollity that seemed to infuse his penmanship? Merely the act of writing itself? I imagined him settling down at his small desk, to the sibilant plea of red-hot fire-brick in the All Souls gas fire, delighted to have a reason to write, blotting and canting, sometimes doubling the stroke or the serif so as to make its blot thicker, fashioning an aphorism only to shoot it down later: Whoever you have a clear view of has a clear view of you. *Vidi est percipi.* Or, this time, hoping for a mastery and concinnity wholly his own, scrawling *Quisquis*, then putting a line through it as he tried *visus videt*, just playing with words, letters, dead tongues. I sometimes imagined him in his lofty chamber, out of the wind, above him a dandelion seed dropping vertical. Or a bookish, epistolary spider.

One conversation we had several times, coming to no agreement. I'd asked him why the word *homosexual* wasn't *heterosexual*, shifting the emphasis from what the homosexual favored to the sexuality he professed. Not a man like self, but a different form of sex. Without a blink or a grin, he trounced the very idea, seeing—granting—my point, but then dismissing it. Therefore, I presumed, the word-makers and word-fashioners in their wisdom had chosen prey over practice, the physical over the categorical? The idea of calling all heterosexuals homosexual must have amused him, but his intimate, finely tuned Greek held him back, making him murmur something about herd instinct without once involving himself in the discussion, although his letters to the newspapers and *Essays in Criticism* (a John Peter essay had fired things off) were as frank and exact about male sphincter pleasures as you had ever read. Different horses for different courses, I thought. Perhaps I had been thinking of those "different" ebullient sluts, the taxed foreigners and freed-women consecrated to Aphrodite or sponsored by Solon, who mainly in Corinth and Athens lived a worldly life denied respectable women, from whom they stood out ("*hetairai*" or "different"), who figured in Attic Comedy and sometimes, like Aspasia of Miletus, persuaded a Pericles to desert his wife for her and her resonant salon. Was I thinking of queens? For sheer outrageousness? Your respectable woman was allowed out with only the equivalent of a sandwich; *hetairai* had *Follow me* imprinted on their sandals.

I had taken to imagining Sparrow as he set out to watch football in Wolverhampton, actually taking a bus to the Oxford train station. He was never, I thought, a proud man; perhaps the sixpence I earned him each term paid his bus fare now and then. I was worth a bus ride to the football train. Arrived, he marveled at the smooth, gliding approach of the train, the step-board only inches above the hard flagstones of the platform, which it never struck. Some image of an immaculate machine age crossed his mind. The intending passenger could step from the station into the train without having to lift a foot, from one dimension spinning at thirteen hundred miles an hour to another capable of only sixty, but therefore 1,360 merely for being a passenger train. As the incoming train slowed and First Class slid to a halt exactly where he stood, as always, he gladdened at the sight of a perched, clean-shaven, fierce wren up in the rafters, chirping the tune of spring. This reminded him of an old Anglo-Saxon metaphor, the Venerable Bede's, in which a sparrow (he thought) flew into and out of a banqueting hall. Thus the image of human life, from darkness into darkness, with only an intervening gaudy amid smoke and cold stones. What was a wren doing in Oxford station, come to see him off? Inside the train, peering through his narrow window, a dining car attendant doubling as a cook saw his haggard, aquiline face melting in a half-smile at the wren and in so doing lost his own most recent thought, of how, when frying sliced potatoes, as you stir the slices, you often see a bit of black that seems an eye unscourged, but turns out to be a space between potatoes against the black of the pan. The forbearing, bushy eyebrowed man awaiting the train cruising to a halt has a wholly misleading stern look when the smile leaves him. He springs into action, boards the train, straight into the dining car, for lunch. The football game begins at 3 P.M. Away he goes to Leamington Spa, Coventry, and Birmingham. Two hours only. A two-hour match. Back in All Souls by dinnertime. A Saturday well-spent, with a wren bonus. He sometimes lingers at station bookstalls, hoping to find his work on sale, but decides a collector of Latin epitaphs had best look elsewhere, near Lincoln's Inn.

I found it absorbing to think of him out on his own, preoccupied with trifles: little green cardboard of the railway ticket; bigger, less rigid ticket for the bus; the British Rail luncheon check, gravy-smudged; the football rattle of a simpler man, which he bought on occasion and left behind him at the ground. Dark suits. Almost a lisped whisper of a voice. A pocket full of sixpence. Over the years, his look of gracious fatigue increased, fanned on by some holy giant in his mind, no doubt a ricochet from the All Souls altar. He did not age, or go gray, but the indoor air that shrouded him seemed less close, and he seemed more alone within his private atmosphere. Perhaps he was drying out, aspiring to a personage in one of his favorite quotations, of which there were thousands: *Anima Rabelaisii habitans in sicco* (the soul of Rabelais living in a dry place). He? No fear: he was closer to the mystical, ingenuous toilers with the delicacy of childhood whom he read on the quiet, then replaced amid the silent turmoil of his shelves. John Sparrow took his pains with sultry civility, like Pater's Marius the Epicurean dropping his football rattle quietly on the terraces in Wolverhampton.

PRINT

For people with not enough to do, Oxford provided various prizes in essay and poetry, but we never paid these baubles much heed. They were for Americans, we said, and those ever-sedulous imports, George Steiner and Donald Hall, competed and cleaned up, coming from a much more prize-conscious culture than Oxford's, where it was almost de rigueur, no matter how well you had done or were doing, to play the whole thing down and actually pretend to have missed the boat in all ways. Stiff lower lip. If you had bowled or batted well that day, it was politic to pretend to be blind and let others do the talking. Thus was the empire built, at the hands of everyone save Winston Churchill, whose prose style accompanied him like a retinue and a festive one at that.

Oxford boasted several journals, none of them in the class of Cyril Connolly's *Horizon* or John Lehmann's *New Writing* or *World Review*, but some of them surprisingly mature, where the vanguard of a new literature tried out its paces. With *Cherwell*, *Oxford Viewpoint* and others, I had no dealings, but *Isis* attracted me with its mix of impure thought and pure gossip. It was the university's newspaper, edited in my time by John Bowen, a gay man with a tanned face of honed bone and deep lines in thick facial skin and a resonant melodious voice. He must have seemed a bit exaggerated to some, but I enjoyed him for his bright wit and his editorial initiative. All he saw from me was poems, for a long time, while I published essays in *Oxford Guardian*, edited by David Hughes of Christchurch (future husband of Mai Zetterling and yet another novelist in the making). The best poetry of the day was Martin Seymour-Smith's, unique I thought for a slinky, sidling movement of slyly chosen words. He wrote unrhymed lyrics in such a way as to make them seem rhymed, his principle of operation being differing degrees of verbal contrast. He and I began a correspondence after he went down, actually to Mallorca to be tutor to the children of Robert Graves. I treasured his eloquent, often rushed letters, knowing they came from a genuine poet who, to make ends meet, had been obliged to go abroad. In later years he wrote an occasional review for *The Washington Post*, an old stand-by of mine, and I always felt pleasure at seeing his name. Did literary journalism swallow the poems, or what? I never knew.

We were a lively, competitive crowd, poets and prose writers mingling: Jenny Joseph, Elizabeth Jennings, Phina Alfrey, James Price, Derwent May, Seymour-Smith, Steiner and I, holding just about weekly parties either among ourselves or to honor visiting writers, and John Bowen and others wrote up the events of each party, selecting *bons mots* and identifying tics and twitches ad libitum. It was fun to find yourself written up the next day, sometimes, for an audience of five thousand, how Paul West stroked visiting poet Lynette Roberts's cony or held Elizabeth Jennings up to a high St. Anthony's window to clear her throat (she had graduated years before and worked now in the local lending library, where I sometimes visited her after going down). I wish I remembered these gatherings better, but they have gone. Sheed or Hall I don't recall at them, or Bush, so perhaps they weren't part of our clique, although they certainly figured in the prow of our literary ship.

Among various student publications brought out by the Fortune Press of London was the annual volume, *Poetry from Oxford*, costing six shillings in dingy brown boards, on the wrapper a prognathous skull wearing a laurel wreath. The one I own runs from "Trinity 1950 to Trinity 1951," and has for its epigraph a quotation from John Dryden: "I am no admirer of quotations." Surely Robert Robinson of Exeter College did not mean that the thirty-five poets represented were derivative plagiarists, but a happier epigraph might have been easy to find. Robinson's emphasis (three poems of his own) was on the creative, as he says in his Introduction:

> Not to provide a critic with a Trend is like stealing a lame man's crutch: it savours of cruelty. But homogeneity cannot be expected among young poets, who have still to develop individual themes; among poets whose art still masters them. All one can hope for is poetry. Which is not to imply that there is an even yield throughout this collection.

Some of the poems have had no more than a whiff, so to speak, of the Muse's apron; others are full. The only discernible unity will be the marks of the beginner—imitation, indecorum, and almostness; but there is plenty of poetry.

Robinson went on to become a television presenter and compère. He writes of applying a close-reading Cambridge standard to the hundreds of poems received ("almost one hundred percent of the residents of the University write verse"), but that didn't work since it seemed to propose a micro-managing of dull material. He then tried the criterion of sheer, unabashed pleasure: delight. Then, let down, he opted for "lucid intervals," which were not too common in the Oxford poetry of my day. He then picks up on what he calls a "prevalent lack of attitude," like a Soviet editor remarking on a curious absence of tractor poems. "I have rigidly excluded," he concludes, "those who believe that analysis of their every mood is as exciting to others as it is to themselves: unless, of course, it *is* as exciting. I wonder what those subjective poets Rimbaud, Villon, Barker, Treece, Gascoigne, and Co. would make of that. As it is, Robinson's own college comes out on top with five poets included, closely followed by St. Edmund Hall and Oriel with four, and Balliol, Magdalen, Wadham, and Lincoln with three. The poet with the most poems chosen is James Price of St. Edmund Hall, with six, and three others with four each. How uncanny to discover a book of poems, an anthology at that, quite without copyright obeisances: we were all brand-new.

Much more captivating, eventually, than copyright were the payment slips sent to us by the BBC (a guinea was a posher version of the pound, favored by tailors, hatters, and bookies as well as other rarefied tradesmen who thought a pound vulgar and also saw that fifty guineas exceeded fifty pounds by two and a half pounds— a lost idiom, a coyness blighted):

Up to and including 8 lines...1½ guineas
Over 8 and up to and including 16 lines...3 guineas
Over 16 and up to and including 24 lines...4 guineas
24-144...1 guinea per 12 lines or part thereof
In excess of 144...½ guinea per 12 lines or part thereof

And this was for only the United Kingdom; overseas in English or in foreign languages was extra. We would soon be rolling in money.

James Price, he of the six poems, entitles his third poem "January, 1951," adding an epigraph from Hoccleve:

Han ye forgote how sharpe it with you ferde
Whan ye were in the werres of Asie?

Then he gets down to it in a tone reminiscent of Auden:

We wait for spring while Europe waits for war.
Will it be this year? Soon, or in late summer?
And will the summer be hot, and the harvest good?
And how many times will we have been in love?

And when will the government fall, or will it fall?
And what chance is there of seeing Italy this year?"

And when the war comes, will it destroy Italy?
Or, more nearly, will there be anything left of London?

There, trapped between unblemished season and the recent blitz, baldly speaks the young Oxford poet of those days, addressing an anxious generation, who perhaps had to wait too long before coming up, but only to accommodate those vets who had to wait five years, if they were lucky, before they did the same. If anything, as the feverishly rubbernecking Trendist Robinson might have noticed, ours was in many ways the Delayed Generation, haunted deep down that their lives—freshman or veteran—were already half over and could only be pulled back by a superhuman effort with calendar and curriculum. Price's other poems in the anthology evoke a similarly drab allegory of the police state, in which life will not be worth living, least of all for the poets. "Police are patrolling the streets of the town," he says; they always have.

What is missing in this anxious poetry is a prosaic thing, already discovered by Auden and Isherwood, Day Lewis and MacNeice: specificity of reference, use of place names and historical names: Vienna, Lidice, and streets and cafés there, statues and graves; Lenin, and Iceland. The young poets of my Oxford generation, having been wounded by history, declined to enter it and cite its saliences. In a way, when Robinson scolds the self-immersed, he is right. History has already laid its lethal paw on them, with bombs and tanks and nerve gas to follow. It would not have been surprising if we had all pulled covers of Swinburne and Spenser and

Blake over our heads and sucked on an opium dream. We had not learned from Yeats either, not even that the texture of modern poetry needs a leavening of names and events in order not to seem hermetic. It is really a matter of allowing what might once have seemed ephemeral to become monumental, as certain names, say, Gandhi, Pol Pot, De Gaulle, even Icarus enriched by Auden, develop almost the richness of modern kennings. We were too ethereal for that, although our retreat into what was then the obligatory study of Anglo-Saxon gave a last gasp to its primitive literature. We helped ourselves to it for epigrams.

If you have watched the Elizabethan and Jacobean poets of England pillaging what they called the matter of Greece and Rome, you will understand that the budding poets of my Oxford generation found recent history so much on top of them that they needed no distant, exotic matter to start them off. Here was history red in tooth and claw (and black and brown if you include Nazis and Brownshirts). What mattered was no fastidious connoisseurship of the remote and mythic, but the snakelike maw of '39-'45 widening to include the Thirties. Perhaps they learned of evil from classicist Rex Warner, at whom, at an Oxford party, the guests had flung empty bottles, a poor welcome to the author of *The Aerodrome* and *The Professor*. No myth was needed of that condemned playground beyond the English Channel; even those who had not witnessed its horrors had a kind of retinitis from it. It is not surprising that most of us drifted sideways, behind Dylan

Thomas, Vernon Watkins, Lynette Roberts, David Gascoyne, Henry Treece, Edith Sitwell and, say, Henry Reed, Celtic or African magic, or even the old Greek and Roman matter: for every Jill or seagull, Robinson's anthology has an Aphrodite or a Ulysses, a Lancelot or a Don Juan. The so-called Movement Poetry that came in next was a gritty, no-nonsense, chiming or rhyming thing, a first taste of minimalism's feeble brush. *Qua* time-capsule, Robinson's selection leaks a certain nostalgic magic, for me certainly, who remembers a good third of its contributors with fresh-stung pleasure, all the more for having put poetry behind me to put on, as Australian cricketers say, the loose baggy. What a serious, groping crew we were.

One of our most interesting visitors was Cecil Day Lewis, who would become my first editor, at Chatto and Windus. Almost as seamed facially as Auden, he stood his ground with an oddly debonair toughness, his hair brushed back in twin tufts as in his photographs: so young a scalp over so lined a face. He spoke gently, counselling us, hearing us out, no doubt recapturing his youthful days with Auden, Isherwood, Spender and MacNeice. He had somehow settled into respectability, what with the Clark Lectures at Cambridge and frequent readings on the BBC *Third Programme*, on which he and John Lehmann presented poems of ours read by Jill Balcon and other actors. The thrill of hearing one's own poems amid those of established poets far exceeded the almost mute terror of hearing (and making) a record of my poems for my parents to hear. I always felt very much a beginner, having no idea that, in order to find my feet, I would have to work my way through poetry, and essays, and a religious crisis, before choosing the elbow room and loose bagginess of the novel. CDL was a tactful, imaginative editor such as we rarely encounter nowadays, and for my novel he got me fifty pounds, less for the book on Byron.

I was becoming, I thought, a very social literary gent, meeting other writers such as Geoffrey Hill, Shaun Macarthy and Gillian Craig, who kept away from the clique or were just not invited. We weren't choosy so much as careless.

Oddly enough, as I recall, our literary parties broadened out (whence the money? *Isis*'s coffers?), and our drab get-up provided a subfusc backdrop to the expensively muted garb of actors and princesses, even socialites, and I recall one evening's entertainment—not much in retrospect—when the centerpiece was John Bowen actually fulfilling a promise to lick Phina Alfrey's arm from pit to tip, and after a while of his almost comical disinclinations she cried out, "You're so *mechanical*, John." And someone else took over, for she was acutely pretty in a flamboyant way, as was Ann Younghusband, whose exact role in all this frolic I never knew. She was not a camp follower, but an Oxford sweetheart. With so many gliterati hanging on, it was only reasonable to expect some of the literati to turn tail and flee the scene. I did not, though I chose my own rather limited company, and I even invited some cricketers in for the evening, with no great success, just to show them how the other half lived. There was never a poets' or writers' cricket team, and what a shambles that would have been, but the games (against nurses or dons) might have achieved supreme lunacy in day-after gossip reports done by Bowen *et al.* I am glad now I never got into that, for there might have been fearful accidents and ruined futures.

After a while, I began to form a near-parodic image of myself, dining at All Souls with the brains trust of the land, and then floating on a tide of South African sherry with presumably the literary inheritors. Was it really that easy? Did privilege alone confer these mingled delights? Or had hard work done it? Indeed, was it anything much at all, to be at Oxford doing these things without doing that much work? I reassured myself that, in previous years, fortified by watercress sandwiches and a cherrywood pipe, I had worked long past the small hours, remembering my father's advice (nothing about sex, of course) to settle in with a good pipe the instant dismay set in. He knew about these things, having been only a boy when he went off to war, younger than I when I first went away from home to nothing more dangerous than a one-inch thick bibliography of English literature printed single-space on both sides. Would I have preferred his war? Would he have preferred my peace? Of course not, but I often mulled over the incommensurate parallel of our young lives, and his imagined injunction: If a shell comes over, cover your eyes quick. The only shells *I* heard coming over were gabby, brilliant wobbly or pobbly middle-aged men who held the university in the palms of their hands. The gods, in mufti.

My father had sat some examination for entry to the local grammar school (an essay question, I suspect), and had won himself a scholarship; but there was no money for his school uniform and schoolbag, and so he volunteered for the First World War as if it were a grammar school and got rewarded for his pains. So, in a professional way, his memory went to waste. He impressed me as Memory even before he had anything much to remember, and at that I was reconstructing his career from long before I was born. What he bequeathed to me, no longer needing it, was his little silver-paper-bound word book, in which he wrote all the words he heard but did not know, presumably to use when he invaded Europe and was at large among the French, say. I still have it, and it has been catalytic in various literary endeavors, his supply of words augmented by my own. Early on, before I went to Oxford, and was seated by the Bush radio (a huge thing) trying to concentrate while he revelled in some symphony, I remember inscribing in those somewhat blood-stained pages such words as "heteroclite" and "opsimath," "nirvana" and "hegira." This little book, no bigger than an address book, must have been between us like the ritual baseball mitt passed from father to son or, to change the idiom, and make it even more personal: a protector to be taped across the groin when at bat.

So much for Father, whom I long suspected of having numb intervals, of which he recalled nothing at all, no matter how momentous had been the events therein. Many things appear for me in album clarity and focus, but catching certain trains, moving into certain rooms, eludes me altogether, as if I were never there—clearly with my mind on something more enthralling. I had blank pages and so did he. These, perhaps, were the ones we wrote words on, for company. I especially remember saying to him I never felt lonely when in the presence of food, which made him laugh, so maybe we felt the same way about words. I see him before me constantly, in the young image that recalls Albert Camus, nodding: I was having a life, he was not. My pianist mother, who some thought had married down by retrieving her childhood sweetheart postwar when he was broken, was the one who urged me on, saying achieve whatever I addressed myself to—a big jump to my slow-developing theory about the use in literature of enigmatic images or "involutes," as Thomas de Quincey called them.

4

TRAPPINGS

NAMES

Life at Oxford was unlike life elsewhere, surrounded as you were by weird traditions (until you got used to them) from the eight-week term to the Latin jargon, from the Newdigate Prize for verse to the custom of sconcing, when the offender has to gulp a yard-long cylinder of beer for talking shop at table, shop being religion, politics, or scandal. Amid such wonders the Oxford accent was always being forged, eventually to amaze the denizens of Wichita, say, or Adelaide, even when the speaker happened to be a corrupted Rhodes Scholar, selected more for athletic prowess than for brains, but you never quite knew. I myself was delighted to run into the Dick Srbs in my own college, whose Nebraska surname had no vowel, but whose almost identical clothing sense prescribed a button-down collar, a bow tie denoting origin, and a natty blazer, drainpipe pants and distinctively American shoes with huge welts, overtooled I thought and weighing a ton (as I later found out in New York City, investing in my first pair). It was just as soothing to observe a contingent of some two hundred all wearing the college's dark and light blue striped tie and/or the similarly striped scarf. These college scarves gave to drab English life the kind of color usually absent, such as would have delighted the Cocteau of *Opium*. Dark and light blue happened to be the colors of my old disreputable school, so I suppose I might have continued wearing the old school tie in Oxford except that old school stripes were broader. I was in my dark green phase then: emerald shirt, similar sports jacket and corduroys, God knows why, the resultant greenhouse effect being to darken my complexion and give me a look of imminent throwing-up. Pale Paul, as friends used to call me, had become nauseous. Perhaps it struck me as a camouflage color, enabling me to go unrecognized in suspicious circumstances. My parents objected, but left me alone to select my style. Perhaps, subconsciously, I was aping the Rhodes scholars (and the Fulbrights, whose sartorial combinations were more hectic while still subdued). It was difficult, in this cosmopolitan surge, to avoid looking a bit of a Cypriot, an Aussie, or a Yank, and I do believe that the foreigners among us began to adopt local styles bit by bit—waistcoats and cardigans they would never have worn at home, and the characteristic lightly tooled English shoe with its thin unwelted sole, its almost dapper uppers, its pointed toe. An observant person would have relished this osmosis of the worn, as the nations blended into one another and (most of all) the open neck tieless and no doubt scruffy came in, all the way from the U. S. of A. No Brit, however, achieved quite the degree of eminent neatness cultivated by the Rhodes boys, whose shirts from home seemed to have been designed exactly to be buttoned down, creating an almost clerical effect with the flanges of the collar actually meeting in front of the Adam's apple, which was to give the illusion of a tie, or at least an enclosed neck, without having the thing on the premises. American clothing appeared designed for strict casualness whereas English tailors mostly insisted on a straitened look, with nothing baggy or spare, no doubt a reflection of national attitudes and historical pride.

"Which side do you dress, sir?" asked the RAF-appointed tailor a few years later as I disappeared into uniform. He was required to ask which side my penis lolled, not one of Oxford's questions at all. Clearly, it was not allowed to hang central.

"Sir, would you please not shuffle, sir?"

Imperative or question? "Half the time," I told him, "I don't know where it is, which side."

"Just so long as it's only *half* the time, sir. Now, may we resume. There is no provision for medium pendulum, as we call it—"

"Or for upright either."

"*Stag sentry*, we say, sir. No, not for that either."

"If you don't mind my saying so, the invention of the trouser, the trews, leaves much to be desired, whereas the codpiece of old helped medium pendulum."

Aghast, he flicked my organ sideways, to dress.

———◆◆✕◆◆———

Was all this blather and trumped-up jargon about genital alignment an orchestrated echo of that often-voiced complaint from wartime, when GIs were damned as "over-paid, over-sexed, and over here"? *Over Here*, as it was said at the time? Was there still some kind of sartorial hangover to come? Had the wars between rough battle-dress (such as even officers wore) and barathea and gaberdine not yet ended? Certainly the Rhodes and Fulbrights had more money than some of us, but not more than the children of the grossly well-to-do, who tended to come up from certain public schools into certain colleges, the child's education a foregone finale. Certain colleges were snootier than others, but there was always a leavening of scholarship boys, whose uncouth accents gave them away, whereas at Lincoln, amid the international rainbow, almost everything passed muster.

One custom I found baffling was the British (public-school) fashion of addressing you by surname only, whereas Americans swooped on your first name and used it relentlessly as if to be rid at speed of a stilted encumbrance always dropped back home. There was something military and stiff upper lip about this surname stuff, as if you were a specimen of a certain stock, from a known or an unknown family, or even a Nazi spy who, after a brief shoddy trial, would be tied to a chair and shot to death before breakfast by a troop of the hardboiled, implacable Scots Guards in a bicycle shed next to the Tower of London. I wondered if the posher youths were this rigid at home. I doubted it, deciding this was the no-nonsense etiquette of public life. So you would hear some such rigmarole as "Srb here will help Stanton to encourage Maddy to walk straight. Understood, gentlemen?" After all, I supposed, wondering how far this trick went, if your name just happened to be Gladstone or Baden-Powell, Churchill or even Jeeves, you wanted to be known and honored, whereas of course most of the surname set had unrecognizable surnames but used them as if they were famous. Ergo, Porky Hooton speaking to Gimblett-Millar might be thinking of those names' reverberations and the history in which their forebears had made their mark. We former grammar-school louts knew nothing of this, and readily joined the unstuffy Americans in their intimate-seeming zeal. Grammar school teachers had certainly gone to surnames, but only in a half-hearted way, no doubt responding sotto voce to the British tradition of using last names lest the personal touch seem like an invitation to see you in your BVDs. Or knickers. In England, a flagging comedian has only to say the word "knickers," with all its connotations of sex and body soil, to win instant laughter and restoration of the hallowed bond between entertainer and entertained.

Thus, murmuring and twanging, first-naming and sur-naming, we mingled together, never actually becoming a college unit (as the well-bonded sports teams were), but enlivened by community, almost a cross-suction (*sic*) of the world, nearly democratic, always affable. Keith Murray was proud of his post-war experiment, being every bit as much a Cornellian as a Lincolnian (Cornell, as I found out later, was the collegium of the open neck, with the knotted tie almost frowned upon. Who there had ever seen

Cornell's pride and joy, Nobelist Hans Bethe, of the Manhattan Project, the man who discovered on the back of an envelope during a train ride from Princeton to New York, how the sun worked, *wearing a tie?* Only once, on receiving his Nobel Prize).

Lincoln in those days was a hearty rather than arty college, outstanding in sports, only to have a next phase of artiness or scholarly esthetics. The English tutor of those days, with whom I had little to do, was Wallace Robson, a rumpled Scot whose rear neck was a home for boils, and I used to wonder if the turtleneck sweater he wore to hide them made them worse. Somehow he seemed to personify the college in its rough and ready ways embalmed in a perfect demeanor. If, as I think, T. S. Eliot in his essays quoted with almost preternatural felicity, Robson had a word-perfect memory for both poetry and prose. Clearly he was at home with every chink and cranny of the body of at least English literature, and I do recall from our one conversation a lively exchange about Stendhal's *De l'Amour*, his lifelong venereal disease, his 170-odd pseudonyms, and his views on therapeutic infatuation. And so to Byron. He was much interested in the sweep and breadth of English literature, which he remembered with passionate detail, as his pupils discovered, as he did its context and provenance. I was the lucky recipient of his Edinburgh lecture on Byron, and was sorry not to have known Robson better.

I wondered why we did not sconce the Bishop of Lincoln for sponsoring religious propaganda during meals. *Benedictus benedicat* ran the Lincoln grace (May the blessed one bless), terse enough but still a clue to the big stick hanging over us, and nothing left for pagans. We were lucky, though, to have anything so pithy and precise preceding our knives and forks. Here, for instance, is a less common grace than the Lincoln one, from Cambridge: *Oculi omnium in te sperant, Domine, et tu das illis cibum in tempore. Aperis manum tuam, et imples omne animal benedictione. Benedic, Domine, nos et dona tua, quae de tua largitate sumus sumpturi, et concede ut illis salubriter nutriti tibi debitum obsequium praestare valeamus. Per Jesum Christum Dominum nostrum.* While this is far from grovelling, it comes close to ingratiation, but why not, since God is the giver of all good things? The Lincoln grace is almost like flicking God on the ear. The longer one translates thus: *The eyes of all hope in you, Lord, and you give them food at the right time. You open your hand, and you fill every living being with blessing. Bless, Lord, us and your gifts, which we are about to receive from your largesse, and grant that healthily nourished by them we may have the strength to owe you due obedience. Through Jesus Christ our Lord.* At this same college, dinner in hall impressed an old member, revisiting, in the following way:

They have self-service, DIY, takeaway snack bars. God knows what now; very informal—Fellows' dinner is still at

High Table, still at a set hour, still has some style; but they have to watch the young get their snouts in the trough yobbo-style any time they like—might as well be a works canteen/McDonalds/any fast food joint.... And at High Table better gobble it down quick or they'll take it away under your eyes, get through your wine quick or you don't get any more. Waiters want to get home to watch *East Enders*, better things to do than feed you. Always like that, but more so now. Guest Night is still civilized, however.

The orotundity of the long grace, never mind how coarsely mouthed, sits oddly with this bazaar; at least Lincoln's perfunctory thing is swift as a guillotine. One is left to elect a mental preference for the old ways or the new vulgarity while the world careens on about its untidy business. How do such preliminary pieties square with the Church-inspired, Catholic-instigated burnings at the stake of Latimer, Ridley and Cranmer in 1555 and 1556, bishops all, for having openly demurred about certain parts of worship, or with the hanging, emasculation, disemboweling and final beheading of Catholics involved fifty years later in the Gunpowder Plot? A mixed-up Church, going recklessly ahead, is something to contemplate while its formulas go on being recited before the soup.

That sconcing rules never worked the other way troubled me, gauche as I no doubt was to think it. They could at least have made the curry better, from superior beef perhaps, given a free meal to atheists. I wondered how the college regarded itself within the maelstrom of recent astronomy, with Fred Hoyle from the distant marshes of Cambridge preaching on TV about the mysterious universe to the pleasure of almost everyone. I am all for lovely even-song, et cetera, but in the interests of pagan delight. It was my father the music-lover who, in a weak moment, confided to me that, often enough, while machine-gunning hordes of advancing Germans, he had muttered or intoned under his breath the chanting of monks he'd gleaned from the after midnight music (wartime was serious) on primitive French wirelesses in Normandy and Brittany. Only the machine-gunner sings to the machine-gunned; it's a practical mat-ter. My father always claimed he would rather have been killing French or Belgians, toward both of whom he had an unruffled but carbolic attitude.

SMELLS

The poet Rilke, to whom my supervisor was introducing me, sometimes concocted theory for its own sake, even in verse. He could not resist the elegant dance of the mind as, like a dog, it pirouetted before lying down. In his letters, he advances a theory of observership:

> Looking is such a marvellous thing, of which we know but little; through it, we are turned absolutely toward the Outside, but when we are most of all so, things happen in us that have waited longingly to be observed, and while they reach completion in us, intact and curiously anonymous, without our aid—their significance grows up in the object outside.

Well, if we can fathom this faltering sentence, its cloudiness offers some interesting insights, and we might purloin it for a theory of our own. He has noticed something commonplace, and tricked it out with Rilkosity. I quarrel with his touch of the anthropomorphic in "things...that have waited longingly." My own view is more mechanical than that, and I sometimes call it, always did, triumphant memory, which is more a theory of perpetual excavation: memories not passively encountered, or eagerly sought out, but allowed to develop in our presence.

Perhaps it is a theory of things' inexhaustibility. There is no end to them. At an extreme, a cooperative soul, assigned to write for an entire life about a fir cone, should be able to do it because, after a while he/she would break through the molecular barrier into all that lies beyond, which the French now define in a university syllabus as ODELA (*au delà*: out there). Give memory room to move about in, "completion in us," as Rilke puts it (or incompletion), and it begins to expand because it is in the presence of a mind. In this way, suitably primed, you regain the odor of All Souls, harder than the smell of Lincoln because of our dominant curry, and thus regain mingled aromas: burning tallow, a sniff of old candlelight; mahogany bruised and smoldering; horsehair in some cushion or other; a compound smell of cooking celery mingled with a smell of damp and undried human skin tinged with a bouquet of shaving soap. All this wafts towards the nose as you read the little visiting-card-shaped slips of paper on which Walter Pater wrote his favorite phrases, no doubt intending to play shuffle with them until he had an imposing sentence beneath his gaze. Shall I say that, recollecting those peaceful days of staring at his slips, this is what came to life in my mind, coming from nowhere else? If, more willfully, you try to assemble these whiffs into one and cannot, but manage to call it Rilke 33, say, as if he owned all nasal effects, you have intercepted the gist of his theory even without succumbing. My own notion of his theory stresses the triumph of memory which, without being pushed or rendered inert, catalytically lets things flower.

That's how the smells of old All Souls come back to me, because there it was peaceful and poorly lit, rather chilly and full of the echoes of strange voices, air that I supposed had lain dormant ever since T. E. Lawrence last breathed it out. Not haunted, but not exactly sterile either. If you really wanted Pater, who remains our leading atmosphericist, you had only to go over to Brasenose College and disentangle his responses from its somewhat hectic, hearty rooms. No teaching, on any regular basis, ever took place in All Souls, which was and is consecrated to research, and perhaps explains its atmosphere, laid aside like an old bugle. A more pretentious scribe might hold forth on the aromas of the souls of thinkers, but I prefer the smell of concentrating men. It's there all right, in the creaks of the wood and the septic hiss of the gas fires, the ineradicable taint of boiling peas, the goblets that once having collected dust never lost it. I look at my old jottings, done during serious mental endeavor having nothing to do with academe, and feel glad. Could one do it blindfolded? Could you be led to Christchurch ("House"), say, or Merton or University, Shelley's old college, and identify by smell? I doubt it, but I never got to know them, and I think most colleges would overlap through their kitchens, whereas women's colleges would confront us with a wholly different palette of scents, from drained-out bathwater headed into the deep bowels of the place to shampoo and scent of civet cat. Someone should be given a fellowship to attempt this. If a smell has memory, then it goes back to the Middle Ages. A smell you have long enjoyed but failed to identify comes to life in a medieval college. Is this what Rilke meant? Bewildered by the world of smell, one journeys around hoping to "place" this or that aroma, hoping to recapture it, or to experience its identity for the first time. It is Platonic to have such smells aboard without knowing what they are of. It is frustrating to be besieged by them, but just as rewarding to wander through a long-unvisited quad or set of rooms and pin them down.

The following are no more than attempts.

An old Bodleian reading room: *Mansion polish.*
An older (Duke Humfrey): ox-blood in the grain.
Christchurch kitchen: wedding cake.
Merton: sour aroma of spilled ink.
Magdalen: deer droppings under bootheels.
Balliol: perspiration and heather.
St. Hugh's: Oxo, Kolynos toothpaste,
    Nivea, Amarny shampoo.
Somerville: Bovril, toast, the obscurer teas.
Corpus Christi: aromas of gardening and cocoa.
St. Edmund Hall: saturated stone and oak fires.

One has to wander much farther than this, of course, equipped with the olfactory version of a Geiger-counter (if such), extending the sortie to May mornings, Commem Balls, potted meat sandwiches by the river, the stench of car exhaust in the High, the mown-grass manicure of the cricket fields. You have to have the nose for it, otherwise you are with Rilke and his theories of animate memory. I somehow believe in all of the planets', even to the tiniest detail, being in constant motion, forever popping up, seeping, deliquescing, shrinking. Brownian and Woolfian motion, everything in a swivet. You can no longer "drive through" Oxford, obliged to take almost meaningless detours. Henry Miller with his taste for *bons mots* amidst the body-blows would have called it an automotive passacaglia. You're better on foot these days, or on a bus. Unless you own one of the stealable bikes always left behind for the next generation, in Brasenose Lane.

Co-ed colleges make for a nasal blur, no doubt helping the sex life along, but sex life always somehow got along whatever the obstacles. Perhaps cohabiting couples use the same shampoo and perfume, or nothing at all, just soap and rubbing alcohol. You certainly can't play the nasal game with the colleges of today, which means something precious and sectarian has bitten the dust. Whoever, on entering St. Hugh's, expected the smell of shaving soap? Well, only those innocents who didn't know about shaven legs, of course, but the emphasis has changed, a tribal nostrum has disappeared. And the near-taboo against the other sex has vanished too. There is no longer the thrill of the forbidden, the option of "getting caught," the lure of Eve in her magic garden of pleats and crannies. My nephew, of Corpus Christi College, sent to Indonesia for inscrutable reasons, returned complaining about the inaccessibility of Muslim women and the constant presence of censorious, iron-clad duennas that no amount of PPP enabled him to elude.

I don't care about this. We had our forbidden things and we loved them. Where all is permitted, and at the new Oxford, most everything is, freedom comes second-hand. If you wanted women, they were there, they always have been. And vice versa. I wonder what this shift has done to the role of nurses in modern Oxford, those nourishers and illicit providers who probably still behave as before, but surely with limited resonance. Perhaps they have taken a back seat or, with the advent of big-league venereal disease, have come to the fore with their special training. They were certainly crucial figures in my day, just as useful with a pound of margarine as in other ways: disabused, blunt, and promiscuous. It can at least be said that the best and brightest men can disport themselves with the best and brightest women now, although that may lead to boredom after a while. Do I hear high-falutin chat from the narrow beds about Walter Benjamin and Lacan? Geezer music once again.

Perhaps the presence of women among men in their private ablutions is a civilizing force, just like marriage. I tend not to believe this, having long ago assumed that men are a different breed: gaseous, impetuous, haphazard, raffish, secretive loners, to be dealt with only on special occasions and certainly left alone when waking up, watching games with balls, or brooding. No doubt this is a boorish view of a fastidious species, an idyllic view of women as vessels of amenity. Perhaps, dumped on top of one another in their most formative years by a university trying in vain to keep abreast (as Cioran says) of the incurable, the same rifts and squabbles as before crop up. I hope so for all their sakes, or the sublime partnership of college foretells terrible disasters in the double bed. In how many years, I wonder, will the denizens of St. Hugh's and Somerville, et cetera head back for their own colleges, newly purged of males, having been informed that ladies perform better in homogeneous groups.

Part of the complex, virtually unpredictable process of "reading" for a degree consists in being left alone. I found it so, having wandered far afield, away from syllabus, even on the stairs of Blackwells or some other indulgent bookshop, ploughing through Pavese, Jünger, Hesse, Kierkegaard, Gide, Bernanos, Mauriac, Jaspers—eclectic as hell as some American Dante told me, but at that point catalytic. I was discovering the subject Oxford did not yet have: comparative literature, upon which I was to fall at Columbia like the veritable bridegroom entering the long-postponed chamber. That was the way to go, as with religion, as indeed in its bare-bones form with Literae Humaniores. Oxford had not realized the full import of its own inventions.

ALIENS

So, as well as writing poems, I was writing essays on foreign authors, unknown ciphers to the Orwell-reading literati with whom I mingled. Myself, I found Orwell drab and ordinary, at his worst as an allegorist, at his best as memoirist: Blackpool's Henry Miller, not a patch on Malraux and Bernanos, Hermann Broch and Ernst Jünger. You see, I was carrying an increasing load of alien touchstones with me, reference to which was not welcome. Rilke my supervisor allowed, but not much else, and he loathed Laura Riding, for obscure reasons. Perhaps she had done him a foul turn in the old days when he was an undergrad at New College, fresh out of Winchester. My French wasn't bad, thanks to our disreputable grammar school and its brilliant women teachers, but my German was based really on my flawed knowledge of Anglo-Saxon. No Spanish at all. I took up the study of Modern Greek, for kicks, having at least a smattering of Greek's old form. I was bursting out all over with intellectual interests, but somehow failed to make contact with Maurice Bowra and Enid Starkie, the very people who would have fed my freakish mind. I tried Edward Thomas, Lincoln's poet, but found him too tweedy, and settled for such as Barbusse instead.

I was still a child of the recent war, and my tastes went that way, inaugurating a lifelong interest in the origins of evil, nations' helpless gravitation towards war, the uselessness of well-meant "Peace in our time" proclamations. The "why" haunted me night and day, especially when I saw how war had ruined my father's life while installing him as an immature hero, a man with overflowing appalling memories to be sipped quietly at the bar among civilized men. I could, should, have been writing about the war poets, whom I kept by me, perhaps sensing that I had registered with the conscription board to enter the RAF when my studies ended. Korea had come into the reckoning and sat there on the fringes of our otherwise juicy lives.

While boning up for the entrance exams to Oxford and Cambridge, I had read my way through the village library's shelf of William Faulkner bound in Chatto and Windus's blue and gold format. I have no idea what he was doing there among chintzy raconteurs, but he wrote English as I had seen no one do it since Shakespeare, and I knew at once that was the way to do it. That seed sat in my skull for the next four years or so, then burst out into my first novel, reviews of which were generous, one of them hailing me as the new Truman Capote, which puzzled me no end. I no longer count that book among my stuff. I went on doing and publishing poems, faintly sensing the big shaggymonster hovering near the frontier, the Faulkner-golem that Geoffrey Bush and John Bowen and the other Oxford proseurs yakked about.

My French held fast, but my German buckled and my modern Greek failed me, so in the end I began reading translations, lapping up such modern Greek poets as Cavafy, Seferis, Sikelianos, Valaoritis, and making interminable notes on them "for later use." One day, I told myself, when my language skills had improved, I would get back to the originals. I read the whole of Gide's journals, Malraux's *The Voices of Silence*, and much of Saint-Exupéry (except *The Little Prince*, a work I have always resisted). But I was not quite ready to open up about Faulkner (I never did until I arrived in Manhattan a couple of years later). If this was a preparation for something big, I never knew. It certainly kept my mind in a ferment while the arbitrariness of rhyme and short lines attacked me from another angle—topic of various conversations with Donald Hall. I thought all meter was arbitrary supposition and I was clearly seeking more elbow room, a less hidebound scope, guided by a vague belief that Oxford prose was sumptuous and luscious whereas Cambridge prose was thin and minimal. I'm not sure I was wrong. Oxford trained prime ministers, Cambridge quantity surveyors, or so I thought.

Yet really, before appraising the difference, if any, between the Oxford and the Cambridge way of doing things in prose, there was the subtle question of what the twin systems had in common. At either place, your tutor was your ally against the assembled forces of the university, all those firsts lined up like the Coldstream Guards to check you out and, if need be, examine you orally. So your tutor might encourage you to do things that would infuriate the examiners: under- or over-write, for example, or get too theoretical when they wanted examples. Just the facts, Jack. Tutors, of course, also functioned as examiners and so knew the ropes pretty well. Maybe there was much squabbling behind the scenes. Ancient rivalries and loathings must have surfaced as well as nepotistic alliances. It was always a gamble, unless the questions made it clear what kind of an answer was required. Presumably, in the best of possible worlds, the questions would be based on the lectures given that year; but sometimes the lecturers would not be the examiners, and sometimes the examiners took pains not to lecture. Talk about a lottery. Compared with the open and much more corrupt system in the United States, where the givers of courses do the examining, this was Russian roulette, and many have gone down the chute because of it. Smart tutors can find out who's examining and tilt their tutorials accordingly, but not all bother to do so, and some tutors thrive in the exalted altitudes of the infinite I Am, never dislodged. One can never really know. The question remains: would an utterly brilliant set of answers, even wrong-headed and opinionated, get shot down? It's possible, just unlikely, but one has heard of scandalous misjudgments (indeed, some have written letters to *Oxford Today* to protest). The entire sentimental notion of one's tutor as one's ally against the world is laudable, and the student may derive a lifetime's enlightenment from it, but he/she may still not gratify the examiners and thus spend a lifetime of discontented illumination.

Why do women do less well than men? What goes wrong? We still have not found out, but the hallowed system seems suspect, and its vaunted impartiality less than that. Perhaps the noblest account of a tutor is W.H. Auden's citation of "Three grateful memories" assembled for Nevill Coghill of Exeter and Chaucer in the epigraph to *The Dyer's Hand*. After citing the grateful three, Auden mentions "a home full of books," "a childhood spent in country provinces," and "a tutor to whom one could confide." Indeed.

Yet what else? Is an Aldous Huxley in English, a Louis MacNeice in Greats, a John Sparrow in Greats, going down to defeat with a second in such a tussle? I doubt it because I believe that eloquence of mind shines through the buzzfuzz of mere information. You can't miss a winner, but also-rans have complained, not to mention women with periods, men with colds, political radicals on the prowl in the wrong arena. I have met them, and the upshot is usually a shrug. The exam is not the day of judgment; but it is for some, and there are geniuses who despair of the pressure cooker.

My sympathy in this goes not only to students, but also to the tutors, poorly paid for going on forty hours a week. The don who took over my supervision when Warden Sparrow became too busy was the critic F. W. Bateson (Freddy) of Corpus Christi: gadfly, pundit, oracle, and wit. Being a geographical Latinist, he called me *Occidens*. I was amazed by how much Freddy took on, even at home in Brill, in Buckinghamshire, out on the lawn with a stack of papers and, to his right, a huge jar such as you find in sweetshops (candystores), full of aspirins, from which now and then he grabbed a handful, eventually of course ruining his stomach. Writing to me after his most recent emergency, he explained the absence of ulcers, adding "it must have been those three innocent aspirins." It was hardly three.

Freddy was a great swatter of wasps, which abounded in his lovely Brill garden, and an uncritical devotee of a rustic radio soap opera, *The Archers*, put out daily by the BBC, in which West-Country folk argiebargied (argued) about the price of turnips and the fertility of bulls. I couldn't abide *The Archers*, but Freddy in his ecumenical way knew the names of all the actors (or voices) and sometimes fidgeted about their fictive fates from day to day. In other matters, such as the wasps, he could be severe, especially on himself; on one occasion he expressed his delight and relief when I praised the prose of one particular paragraph for its *slatelike* qualities. Without being a fuss-budget, he worried nonstop about his charges (tutees) without ever becoming sentimental about their chances. He did his all and that was that. Eight hours daily of relentless scrutiny and impromptu brio did not seem to tire him, and he had only the merest interest in food, hardly even looking at it, allowing just anybody to order for him. He called food fuel, but seemed to wish his students ate more of it. His wife Jan was a magistrate—and could be severer than Freddy; God help offenders. Freddy signed himself "FWB" and communicated mainly by postcard. He had only recently been made a Fellow of Corpus, which shows you how fast Oxford moved.

It was Bateson the bountiful who recalled me from Canada to take up a position in University Park, Pennsylvania. He himself, to make ends meet, had taken occasional visiting appointments in the States, more or less to his taste except Berkeley. Compared with his habitual forty hours a week, I thought. My own assignment, he joked, would be very congenial.

"Lecturing on Shakespeare," he said, "to an audience of some six hundred. You have a nice voice."

"*Shakespeare?*"

"They won't know the difference," he told me. "You have the right accent. That's all that matters." And so it turned out. Later that year I opened with *Titus Andronicus*, much to the students' amazement. They had never thought Shakespeare could nod, or know that much Latin. If only they could have seen the movie, that impasto of noir and fatuity, they might have seen the play in a less judgmental light.

"Well, Occidens," he'd say in that Oxford manner, "how goes it?"

"He comes across as one of our most amazing essayists. Shakespeare, I mean."

Bateson chuckled. "I dare say whatever you tell them is news. Such a new country, this. They just about worked me to death at Berkeley. They're kinder here, less Teutonic. That so?"

It was, but I thought some of my six hundred students wanted to lynch me for mocking the Bard.

"Let them," he said. "You have a sturdy neck."

I could see now that, in his genially puckish way, he saw me as some kind of corrosive life-form wished upon my students by a malefic power across the pond.

"Do you play tennis, Occidens?"

"Never, not since my teens."

"Well, I do, and I've noticed how many young Americans overtax themselves on the courts and drop dead of a heart attack or something. Almost an American tradition. You never hear of our tennis players doing that."

"Aha," I told him, "it must be the brown sauce they take with meat that toughens them up." He gave me a drab, puzzled look and walked away, slapping his racquet against his knee. Right out of P. G. Wodehouse, I thought.

So add Bateson's summons to University Park as yet another of Oxford's generous acts, no questions asked, none answered. That was one side of Bateson. Another was harder to figure. On one occasion, having sorted out his papers, mainly letters and manuscripts from poets and novelists as well as letters from fellow critics, he burned the stuff from the creative people and kept the critics. Amazing. He kept you on your toes, and kept telling me I should now edit a Shakespeare play, where the money was.

In the United States and Canada, of course, where I've done my teaching, a winner surfaces fast, certainly by the end of the second of four years, his/her grades known, the reputation virtually made. Who is going to shoot such a person down at the end? There is not even the mechanism to do it with because a student will carry the same course load throughout, ending as he/she began with maybe two or three courses (yet not necessarily in the major, so it's *possible* to mar one's record with a B in compulsory swimming or something just as foolish). By the same token, the American/Canadian student knows nothing of that agonizing corrida the finals ("Schools") week that ends three or four years' work: more than half a dozen exam papers in five days. That's the killer, and if you can't stand the pace, the fever pitch, you've had it. I am thinking of several excellent students who didn't have the stamina, and how their careers fared afterward (one of them married the senior professor of English and that, in its ludic fashion, took care of that). One fellow put his neck on the railroad line. Another jumped in front of a bus. Another, poorly in the vital week, didn't come up to snuff. The only person who can relish such a system is the opportunist, maybe good officer—or Navy Seal—material, who can bring to bear just briefly a ferocious, mordant energy never seen again.

PROSE

I am trying to work my way toward a definition of Oxford prose, not merely exalting the lush flummery of the Sitwell family, but taking Edith's study of Alexander Pope seriously (meticulous examination of his line vowel by vowel, consonant by consonant) and relating that shrewd glare to F. R. Leavis's exact, almost pedantic scrutiny of Wordsworth and Keats in *Revaluation*. These are perhaps not the names you might expect, since Edith tends to gush and Leavis is one of those Cambridge fanciers of the loupe. This is not a matter of who's in and who's out; the pursuit of Oxford prose goes everywhere of course, like the pursuit of the *Graf Spee*, and we have to pick up helpful hints and timely examples wherever we can. The general idea abides, however, of prose as a malleable, idiosyncratic idiom geared to the profundity and plenty of the world, which I think some Oxford writers—Pater, say—have constantly addressed themselves to, hoping perhaps to match those qualities in their words, and to stir in their readers a similar awe. This has nothing to do with the plain prose touted by the Royal Society's committee of twenty-two, nor with the minimalism of so many American practitioners who, turning their back on Faulkner, scant the luscious world at hand as mere contraception.

One important difference between what I am calling Oxford prose and Cambridge prose is that the former not only spells out the magic of being, but sometimes explains it whereas the latter fixes mainly on explaining, so the one is sometimes like voodoo whereas the other is a mere recipe. Both may well be articulate, but the lusher, more lavish kind tends to shove articulateness where man has never gone, hoping to enact a spell. And this is what the Oxford writers do—I am not speaking geographically here although this is more an Oxford tradition than, say, a Dublin or an Edinburgh one. The writers I have in mind would be Ariada Mencken, Thomas Carlyle, Julio Cortázar, Lawrence Durrell, Janet Frame, William Gass, Malcolm Lowry, Thomas Macaulay, Bradford Morrow, Rabelais, Nathalie Sarraute, James Hamilton-Paterson, Dylan Thomas, John Vernon, Robert Coover and quite a few more. These are the practitioners of thickness. I find this dark-blue/light-blue shorthand convenient not because the dark blue teaches future prime ministers how to write thickly, nor simply to switch Lowry from one university to the other, but, say, to distinguish Persian rugs from matting. One does not strive to enter this rather precious club; one is born into it, and one's personality confirms the birthright. If I say purple, it means the best of purple, as in the richest runs of prose in such a novel as Beckett's *Watt*, say the long divagation about the mailman Arsène.

Of course, this kind of writing transcends anything political, having more to do with what lies beyond the doors of perception than with what's in the larder, though even some kinds of bread are richer than others. I am concerned with revelation, not that I am claiming my time at Oxford opened up all doors for me or that I had never known until then that there could be such writing as what I'm calling Oxford writing. Perhaps there never was, never will be such a thing, but it's what you might expect from Oxford with its unpuritanical zeal, its addiction to the flounce and the swirl and Michael Jackson. To find it, hope against hope, we might go back to Swinburne and Ruskin, Jeremy Taylor and Sir Thomas Browne, even Nashe and Traherne. It is the kind of prose that shows up only intermittently, and the no-nonsense English tradition is against it because the English don't seem to like their authors to have too much fun. It is there, though, reminding readers that the universe is not merely steam and clockwork, that we do not have to fathom a mystery in order to write about it. So I detect, as well as the Oxford I attended, an Oxford of the mind, the heart, subtly insinuated among dreaming spires, and always available provided there are minds to revel in it.

I have been told that I had a scuffle with Donald Hall at the top of a staircase somewhere in Oxford. If this is true, it was brave of me because he was both taller and heavier than I, yet perhaps not as muscular. I don't recall the event. *Genus irritabile*, writes Horace, speaking ill of poets such as himself (and novelists too).

The poet who amused me most, making me think he'd changed his name by deed poll just to make an entrance, was John Donne (Jack), whose real name this was, and priceless to boot, giving everyone pause until they twigged he was not a holy sonnet reading itself aloud. He had in his time been close to one of our lady poets, and then he ditched her for someone else, as was his wont. It happened every day.

NEBULA

When a group of almost like-minded people is as privileged and committed as ours was, it is not surprising that they join and part in a kind of magnetic motion, always able to retreat back into the group, able to surge outward into a new relationship because being in one wasn't that far from still being within the group. Your main connection was with the group anyway, and one would think so firm a bond would endure well into adult life. With a few of us it did, and one might actually then catch up with someone belatedly, like Lotte Zurndorfer or John Brownjohn, a poet and a translator who somehow had not gone down the chute of nine-to-five work (Eliot-style ten to three). I ran into June Barraclough in Foyles bookshop in after-years, just before she went off into the Air Ministry to a post well below her intellectual capacity, in spite of having a relative who held a chair of modern history in another university. It began to dawn on me that the women were not thriving as Oxford women should, and I wondered if that was because they hadn't made contact with Oxford women who had done well already. Did nepotism really go on? Of course it did. Because of it, or in spite of it (sheer ability will out), John Bowen, after journeying to Ohio State on the same boat as took me to Columbia, became editor of *The Sketch*, a glossy, and Derwent May joined *The TLS*. Elizabeth stayed on at the Oxford library and Martin went to the Graves Commission in Mallorca. Alvarez, having come and just gone, had joined the *New Statesman*, which took me on too as a fiction reviewer and then, in the loosest manner imaginable, air correspondent when I mustered into the RAF to do my compulsory national service at long last after seven years of delicious dawdling. We were scattered, although the poet Edward Lucie-Smith appeared one day in the RAF, easily identified by any Oxford man, and Steiner had wafted away to *The Economist*. Other Americans, Bush, Hofer, Sheed, Bartlett, Stanton, Maddy, Srb, Bartlett and Walsh had all returned to their native heath (I kept in touch with the last two), yet not without having vehemently urged me to apply for a Smith-Mundt scholarship stateside (which I learned to say without slurring it). Actually, Yardley and I lasted longer than almost any of them, fudging up this or that pretext for staying on, although registering a faint displeasure of obsolescence as the college filled with strange faces. Yardley went to Teddy Hall, I to Columbia, and the phantasm of the brimming choirs was just about over. I had the dreadful sense of: Been here and never noticed it, which we all felt to some degree, having been overpowered by the secular at the expense of the eternal. Yet something magical and august had taken root: not just happiness, though that was certain, but a feeling of having at times become as old as Oxford itself.

Attempting over the years to articulate this excellent sensation, I can only adduce a piece of music: the blind Rodrigo's *Concierto de Aranjuez* familiarly played by brass bands as "Orange Juice," which has always made me feel as old as Spain, slinking through an endless doorway, awed by ancient atmosphere, rejoicing at all the souls alive in the same place where other souls no longer are. Some music—Elgar, Vaughan Williams, Finzi, Bax, Delius, among the locals can do this, but also Villa-Lobos, Ravel, Debussy, Fauré, de Falla, Chopin, Scarlatti, Hindemith, Prokofiev (I bow to a superior art as my mother always said I would)—provides this haunting, overwhelming sense of historical spread or elongation, evoking the quite serious comparison of astronomers, who tell us that a cat dropped into a black hole will end up as stretched-out linguini. When I hear those sounds, I have ancient Blakean feet, and nervous genes, knowing how little a part of anything I truly am, even though I dream on grandly. Some literature can do this to you (De Quincey, say, peering into the Great Orion Nebula and frightening himself to death), but not much. Literature allows itself to be too secular because mercantile elements fancy they control it, and only the most arrant writers disobey.

5

IDEAS

SADNESS

Light years away from my official studies, it was at Oxford that I began my quest for the sadness motif in literature (as in music too). Perhaps I was hunting the obvious, but it didn't feel so. My notion was that, to people who had not even professed to be readers, something seeped down to them warning that serious art (music or literature) was bound to depress. There was no way in which it could possibly deflect them from the fact that, sooner or later, the human condition would sever them from all they held dear and annul them forever. The question, I supposed, was how to write serious art without revealing, even using as a bedrock, this appalling fact. If you are Gilbert and Sullivan, or Wodehouse, merchandising gaiety, then you will get away with your frolic; but if you are Beckett, Gogol, Eliot, Kafka, Proust—the list is miserably long—you will keep on running into this problem. It is wise of Milton to propose justifying the ways of God to man, but to do so may well involve you in rationalizations of supreme casuistry. If there is no escaping the facts, what can serious literature do that is both worth having and honest? Not very much, I was afraid. It came down to truth versus entertainment, or something like that.

Could it be that, thanks to some compact between authors and readers, we would pretend to be jolly even while readers knew the real truth? Were we willing to be taken in just because the real, inescapable truth was so awful?

Perplexed by these unsavory thoughts, I wondered at the paradox of it all. Why did we need literature at all if all it could give us was misery? Was the prospect of delight with our loved ones so enticing that we did not care about the destroyer of delight waiting at the other end, chopping some of us off short even? What was there in life but a temporary anodyne in the face of the final quietus? I thought such things mattered even to those who "took life in their stride," heedless of ultimate consequences, but there seemed few hedonists among serious readers. Could it then be that readers, come what may, needed to have their noses rubbed in the presentation of things at their worst, what the Greeks called *deinosis*? Was the final *coup de grâce* so awful that we could hardly believe it and therefore needed a continual diet of misery-confirming conclusions? If serious literature is ghastly, why not ignore it, do without it? I detected a strong streak of masochism in the dear old reader, who wanted to have his cake even if it killed. Surely this was an odd thing. Yes, the public, even the discriminating one, went for Gilbert and Sullivan, say, but they also fed on corruption and death. Surely this was an interesting folkway, best summed up as benign torture.

What I found hard to believe was that people stood by serious art even if its message was frightful. Could it be that humans were subtle sophisticates who managed to balance *deinosis* with delight, siting literature in between the two, able to revel in the texture, say, at the same time as intuiting the worst? If so, this was a clever trick about which the anthropologists had written too little. Where in Levi-Strauss and Lévy-Bruhl did this come up? Was it a mythic habit we took for granted? Knowing full well what literature would do to us, we got on with the job of appreciating it, and that was that. Was this not a freakish paradox living alongside the ever-open faucets of entertainment in our culture? I was always being amazed that serious literature kept on being written, though not half as much of it as one might suppose. Why bother? Its message was never new, had not changed since Donne's sermons or Hieronymus Bosch. Could it be, I wondered in the very vein of the serious academic writer, that our taste for morbidity was never satisfied, and we wanted to witness all the variants of hell on our own nerves? If so, were we not an exceptional species? Or was I missing something? All these cheerful readers of the worst had faith in some kind of afterlife. That must be it. They looked forward, as did the ancient Egyptians, to an afterlife that duplicated life here on the planet. Yet many of the serious readers I knew had no such afterlife in view and, like heroes and heroines, faced extinction without a tremor. Why were they reading serious literature? Because they did not believe it? Hardly. Were they not like some incessant readers of books about the Holocaust, who could never get it through their heads how abominable it had been?

In fact, I was looking at the act of reading itself, and shuddered to think what would happen to us if we ever gave it up in euphoric despair, or something such. Serious writers, I contended, should write about serious, "last" things, but not expect anyone to read them. It was not true: they were indeed read, which argued, at least as I saw it in my greenhorn days, an extraordinary manipulation of the image. What confronted us time and again, from Dante to Genet, was literally dreadful, but we somehow responded to the esthetic initiative that looked it in the eye and transformed it into living prose. This was not merely getting used to the bad, it was converting it into something palatable that enabled us to dance on the rim of hell. And all the truth about loss of life, of loved ones, somehow passed us by while able manipulants made their best of it, like Hamlet or Byron fingering the texture of death and thriving by simply having managed to do it—not being inert or caught without an idea that enabled you to fight back even on the plane of figurative language.

Astounding. Then how had literature survived without anyone's noting the paradox of it all? Aristotle of course, who knew everything (as Beckett says), but nothing else, had dealt with tragedy to an honorable reception; but did his theories of purgation and purification, so long rehearsed, apply to the novel, say? I doubted it, and Humphrey House's little Aristotle primer, while neat and pretty, hardly made the matter any clearer. We were not an audience massed together; we were isolatos, readers scattered haphazardly across airports and housing tracts, on toilets or falling asleep. We were *dissipati* in the sense the Spanish navy facing Drake had been. So, as readers not much communicating with other readers, we were functioning in some existentialist privacy quite separate from the concentrated community of theatergoers Aristotle had in mind. To him, the live show was the all.

ENIGMAS

Hearing the tenderest, most yielding passages of Elgar's *Violin Concerto*, I had an inescapable feeling that, contrary to certain suppositions I'd had that evening when entering the auditorium, all was right with the world, as if the orchestra had played the music—animating it—right back into the universe's central core, wherever that was. Dreams were going to be fulfilled merely because music had become their metaphor, Elgar their catalyst. If the most precarious emotions could be voiced so gently amid the harshness of the world, not patterned as some maintained after the harshness of stars, what could be wrong? The destructive element contained the joy of man's desiring. But only as a vulnerable capsule, a cherished exhibit of no small discernible influence in human affairs. I was discovering the pristine abstractness of music, which, seeping out of the world back into the world, had nothing to do with us except during performance or in the hands of devout score-readers. This riddle occupied me long and generously, becoming the riddle of acute sensitivity, an *ignis fatuus* among the sullen rages of history.

The next stage in my literary excursion followed logically from the outset, although few of my contemporaries got my point.

I was out on my own, like Wordsworth, whose *Excursion* was more mystical than mine. I was accustomed to that feeling, however, and I was at Oxford because of it. To me it was original thinking perhaps best saved for an All Souls dinner.

If accurate literature merely saddened us, then why bother with it at all instead of playing snooker, darts, or roulette? If, in spite of all, we still craved its awkward frisson, did it not follow that we also homed in on such of literature's tricks as De Quincey's "involute": "a compound feeling incapable of being disentangled," or what I called enigmas. Enigma was not that far from the code-breaking scramble of the recent war, when boffins, crossword experts, and senior wranglers (as Cambridge called its top mathematicians) gathered in a country mansion as if starring in an Agatha Christie movie and bit by bit broke the German code and the Nazi heart. Life, it seemed to me, then and after, was full of runic messages, at least according to the De Quinceys. Literature made us unhappy, reminding us of the irremediable, and some enigmas baffled us to death, actually forming a synecdoche (when a part stands for the whole—*head* for *cattle*). Death was the ultimate enigma to which writers addressed themselves, so we could deal with death at one remove by dealing with its counterparts, as Kafka, Beckett, Conrad, and even Dreiser and Wharton did. Yet Oxford's system or rigmarole forbade researching such notions and preferred matter-of-fact compilation, thwarting lively young minds that, thinking such thoughts, felt close to the self that had confronted the scholarship exams not that long ago, responding eagerly to the heady invitation to think hard for three hours. The gate that let you in took you to a dead end whose keepers, most of them, kept you dryasdust as they, while just a few of them—the All Souls crowd, none of whom taught although they lectured—let you loose. It became clear that teaching dons held you back even from your own cleverness while sinecure dons did the opposite. Virtuosity led you straight to tedium, and tedium, I supposed, to a job. Who then concocted those ebullient, suggestive scholarship exams? There was a piece missing from this scholastic jigsaw puzzle. If the examiners were high-spirited, why were the tutors so staid? Why were the final exams (Schools) so stodgy? I never found out. To do so would have required a full-scale survey of cooperative witnesses and a uniform account of variables. I was only looking at the English faculty anyway, and who knew what went on in philosophy, chemistry, or law? Truth was, I should have enrolled in French, if allowed to, thus encountering Starkie the pioneer of Rimbaud studies and Bowra, whose *The Heritage of Symbolism* had seemed like Ali Baba's cave on my first reading. Their take on literature seemed close to mine, compatible with the likes of me.

Here, for example's sake, I concoct one of those early scholarship papers for a mythical Oxford college, doing it from both memory and imagination, with a fond smile at the questions I might have attempted in that cloud-cuckoo-land of aspiration.

St. Lampeter's College, Oxford
Sir Philip Sidney Scholarship in English

Attempt ONE or TWO questions.   3 Hours.

1. "Just as verse is merely prose curtailed,
   so prose is verse extended." Discuss.
2. "Pope is to Dryden as Donne is to Cowley."
   Discuss.
3. What is satire? Illustrate your answer.
4. Can surrealism exist? If so, for whom?
5. Discuss Tennyson's view of Maud.
6. What, to English writers, was the matter
   of Greece and Rome?
7. Compose your own obituary as written
   by George Bernard Shaw.
8. Does Chaucer lack anything?
9. What is your notion of (a) A Silver Age,
   (b) A Golden Age, (c) An Age of Anxiety?
   You need not refer to Greek or Roman
   authors exclusively.
10. Is there such a thing as female prose?

So: I had official sanctioned studies and well-nigh forbidden ones. I was only too ready to prate about surds ("deaf root" in Arabic), how the enigma surpassed both allegory and symbol. Allegory, in which one thing equalled another, was Henry James's story "The Beast in the Jungle," about John Marcher who kept waiting for the beast to spring out upon him, but eventually realized the wait itself was his portion. Behold a didactic allegory. Symbol was Virginia Woolf's melodious waves, both radiant and propulsive, handily defined and dealt with, yet ineffable at source. Behold the complex fringe of a mystery, almost as unknowable as Rilke's angels. And enigma? Less to do with Elgar's *Variations* than with Beckett's Molloy who, while straddling his bicycle, hears a voice demanding his papers. He produces a few slices of newspaper he carries with him for visceral emergencies. Or Byron, even, coming up with his own phrase "the spoiler's art"—which I later purloined for my book on him. He felt bound to ruin the thing he loved.

Enigma, I fancied in those novice years, approached the Zen *koan* and reduced humans to aghast dubiety, confronting them with a world that just did not make sense, an *aperçu* that André Breton in his novel *Nadja* revised into, "Life has to be deciphered like a cryptogram." The line of succession from De Quincey to Beckett was plain, supplying a parallel to what R.W. Chambers called the Continuity of English Prose—I mean the continuity of British bafflement, to which I nowadays add Maurice Blanchot, William Burroughs, Osman Lins the Brazilian, and Alain Robbe-Grillet. I was increasingly interested in how literature—the best literature— reintroduced us to death in a different guise, more palatable perhaps, but no less mortifying: death devolving into a motif we barely understand. As in Beckett's *Waiting for Godot*, say, or Boris Vian's Schmurz figure in *The Empire Builders*, his on-stage inflated whipping boy.

I began to wonder in my off-hours if anyone had ever tested things that made sense against things that didn't. Yet how test peristalsis against death? Could it be that we enjoyed enigmas because they trained us, schooled us in enigmatics, at which we were never good? Our entire educational system taught us to make sense of things, sometimes too much so, especially when coping with works of art. Detective fiction enthrones the sense-making flair of course, and science fiction teases it, proposing natural combinations hitherto unknown, but standard in any world based on silicon.

HOOPS

Thus ran my partly enlightened mind, picking examples at random, wondering if in John Keats's *Hyperion* the decline of the old gods, moaning and kvetching, taught us about death, exposing an entire process of obsolescence and decay, or merely epitomized that process in a juxtaposition: old versus new, with nothing more to be said. Somehow, Keats manages to do both, perhaps because his depiction is abstract and mythic and therefore processively terse.

You can smell the young man coursing through the hoops that Sparrow flinched from. Was I not discussing a real problem at all, but only a verbal puzzle, a logomachy? Was this why Oxford, with its centuries-old experience of evading unanswerable questions, shoved us away from them toward minor textual matters? Certainly, in its ecclesiastical role it had grappled with the Jesuitical whys and wherefores and trained young minds to have faith rather than beat their brains uselessly against cosmic enigmas. Oxford *knew*. Or, rather, Oxford knew how to leave well enough alone, shelving such theological matters as its divines eschewed. Old Greats was as close as the nascent thinker could get to "last things," and even then the ingenious/ingenuous questions of Plato had a cut-and-dried air, settled long ago: Yes, Thrasymachus, but if A be true, then does it not follow that B.... All that softly, softly, catchy monkey stuff seemed old hat.

So I never figured out why serious literature, so depressing, lured us on, or why ready-made enigmas helped us in the encounter. It was true that trivial literature left something out and thus always seemed a doily. We shied away from it and aimed at Oxford's serious thinkers from another age: Pater, Ruskin, Arnold and Newman. Of course we did. Theirs was the big league of metaphysical discomfort, and their answers somehow had more heft than those arrived at in our own century by Aldous Huxley and Bertrand Russell. The only Oxford thinker who had a nineteenth-century flavor was C. S. Lewis, my encounter with whom came later. I wrote off our absorption with "high seriousness," as Matthew Arnold put it, to masochism or helpless obsession. Someone from another, deathless planet might have marveled at our outrage over death, but understood it as indignation at a wholly redundant transit, a quirk in the fabric of local evolution. Galileo, I recalled, said death was necessary to accommodate the new-born: a local saw, of course, far from apt if people lived forever.

Perhaps it was the jocund reinforcement of Oxford's bells that fostered such lugubrious wonderings. In a secular university, such as Columbia, I would not have had such thoughts (and did not). It was Oxford's antique affiliation with faith that stirred me to morbidity and set me thinking on yet other lines.

Disease, preliminary to death, I began telling myself, was nature's form of art, mutilating, infesting, aborting, akin to our own movement of expressionism, which stressed not what was "there" but how you felt about it. Unappeased nature ruined millions with ease, then killed them. Was this not a savage spectacle, easily surpassing expressionism in both severity and volume? It was an artform designed to please nobody, but just to be. Oxford, the paragon of good will, charm, and piety, the city of dreaming spires, was feeding the metaphysical rebel, but the wise men I now and then dined with had put all my "last things" behind them, no doubt with relief, but in a mood of regained anxiety signalled jovially to me over the blackberry tart that they understood, thought it good to articulate such stuff while young. Meliorists all, except Berlin, whose very pobble hid some sense of the appalling forced into a back seat in the interests of amenity.

DISTANT VIEWING

What a sitting duck I was for Sartrian hard tack. A behavioral grammar of arrant self-assertion (or self-definition) did not appeal to me, but where else to go? I picked up a lecture, "Existentialism is a Humanism," in which Sartre told how during the war a young man had approached him, obliged to choose between staying in Nazi-occupied Paris to tend his grandmother, and joining the Free French in London. Would Sartre choose for him? Sartre does not say what he advised, rather coyly confiding that he already knew what the young man had decided to do. How evasive, I thought: the high priest of decisive, excuseless self-assertion skulks in the shadows of shyness, mocking us with the rigor of his mind. After dismissing the politicism of Camus (making political noises without assuming a political stance), I soon slunk back into estheticism, or rather the mangled nature that mangles us. *Mangle*: the very word evoked the laundering process in which the mangle (a wringer) squeezed water from wet clothes. There was even an art to that. Alas that the best expressionism was German, with an occasional Norwegian thrown in.

After a bout of publishing essays in such religious periodicals as *The Hibbert Journal* and *The Plain View*, and such literary ones as *The Adelphi* and *Window*, and placing poems with *World Review* and James Reeves the blind editor of *Quarto*, I began to fidget for elbow room. The novelist was stirring again and would in the next few years embark on an allegorical novel I eventually destroyed. I had come out from under the cold compress of Oxford piety and convention. I was reading Pater and Malraux, amazed by how much their views of art overlapped. And T. E. Lawrence, whose name never surfaced at All Souls, and Georges Bernanos the French Catholic who wrote on paper set between knife and fork on the kitchen table. I no longer heard the bells or attended parties. A genuine seriousness had replaced my hectic dis-orientation and the dull old hoops dreaded by my supervisor had spun away. Only one remained, the one requiring us to have an atti-tude to the universe. Why? I have no idea, but perhaps for pride, swank, self-respect. I had now discovered Thomas Mann with his *"I do not much believe in belief."* At the familiar conundrum "How did the physical universe produce mind?" my mind stopped. What a strange mess for matter to get into. Evolution, just as puz-zling as ever, seemed just another Just-so story. Take it or leave it, it will get you in the end.

I go back to Freddy Bateson's oft-repeated confidence that while he admired the writing of *King Lear*, he could not bear to watch the play. I doubted if he could bear to read it either, but I wondered if, reading some putative novel of the play (Jane Smiley's *Thousand Acres* would come along much later), he would be more receptive, granted that the experience of solitary reading is a more private, interruptible siege with no audience, no actors, and often an interfering omniscient narrator. Aristotle's notion of vicarious horror endured in some kind of homeopathic trance would not appeal to Freddy, nor would the notion of pain refined by proxy. The exact difference between drama and fiction (an actor feigning onstage and an abstract narrator overhearing) is hard to state, but clearly the fictional version is less intense, less of a piece, more subject to what the CIA was going to call "distant viewing," when through telepathy an observer in London can "see" things going on in Paris. Plays are made of talk and action; novels of unheard voices and unenacted action. A novel's dialogue is for the eye, and this makes an enormous difference.

Imagine the twenty-year-old literary tiro grappling with all this while scanting his own distant viewing of a Nineties journal. I wrote down only scraps, salient portions that leopards reject, somehow knowing I would return to last things in an ampler, less strenuous time. I am happy to have those evocative remnants of an old mania seen, now, through the eyes of a novelist whose passion for narrative does not fade. No one, half-twigging Aristotle without ever *being* him, is ever going to plumb those imposing saws. There is room for a study testing catharsis against empathy or, as I recall from my earlier worries, the role of misery in drama against its role in the novel. What draws us to inflict damage on ourselves, as if the human condition were to improve, might be a furtive desire to see what art could make of such intractable subject matter. I used to think so, and sometimes still do, favoring the esthetics of *deinosis*. Out of the drab and drear comes forth sweetness? I wonder.

I would never ape Freddy Bateson's passion for aspirin, but I learned from him how to trap and kill a rat or swat a wasp, as well as something about the metaphorical nature of all theology. We, he and I, were the unbelievers who found metaphor holy in itself, which was to say metaphor as human transcendence at its best. While Freddy devoted himself to editing *Essays in Criticism* with Christopher Ricks, and teasers such as "the shortest way out of Manchester," I marveled at the scenic counterpoint of Berlin's written English, sharp contrast to the researchers who infested the Duke Humfrey reading room and other precincts of the Bodleian Library. I toyed with the idea, no doubt filched from Ernest Hofer (Oxford, Yale, and the Sorbonne) of arranging for some freshman to enter all of Oxford's male colleges at the same time, *in statu pupillari ubique* (pupating everywhere), who would then rise to fame on a series of astute comparisons broken down into food, curfew, dons, mod cons, graces at meals, heads of colleges, matrons, firsts, foreigners, and so forth. For one year perhaps. What a pregnant contingency sample that would be, better by far than any Oxford anthology done by adult hands.

I am amazed by how much I took Oxford for granted, surely gob-smacked by many of its ways, but oddly at home, not because I had read about it, as I had, but because I had already had my Oxford during the ritual of entrance examinations and the ensuing pause. It was usually a two-year delay. In the interim, with a scholarship in hand, I imagined what "going up" was going to be like. I had already chosen an Oxford award over a Cambridge one, and I knew what I wanted: gowns, candies, roaring fires; all clergymen who played squash; rosy-tinted libraries in which ancient scholars hung fire; deer, ducks, and bells; ramshackle bicycles called "grids"; quads, scouts, and bullers, dark blue boat races, huge arriving cabin trunks full of brand-new Irish linens; marmalade and porridge for breakfast, old stones and older tombstones, chamberpots atop the martyrs' memorial; Shelley, Waugh, Aldous Huxley, Pater and Sir Thomas Browne; port wine, multicolored scarves, furrowed Balliol brows, porter's lodges, and that interior yellow glow of evening lamps discerned by an adolescent cycling by with Jean-Jacques Rousseau in his pocket, unseen by the elect at their oaken benches as they sat in the laps of the Middle Ages to get their fill of Greats. I hungered, at least in the abstract, for moral tutors (whatever that meant), cheery Fellows of colleges, all of old Oxenford. What a preposterous pipe-dream, but it gave me Oxford before Oxford arrived.

Hagiography indeed, much of it lost in an older youth's impetuous cling to the eventual Oxford, hardly part of any such idyll, cranked sideways by Yanks and veterans and the terminal moraine of Glenn Miller's orphaned neatly machined orchestra. The world had moved on, winced back to normal, almost, and, if anything, had become, because more dilapidated, more ancient than ever. Winston Churchill had come and gone, honored like a passing pope, put out to grass without sentiment or ceremony, and the newspapers were full of rationing, "austerity," and Sir Stafford Cripps, the ascetic of economics. D-Day was only five years back, and England was broke.

6

SOULS

Conversation with Keith Murray
Rector of Lincoln College
Summer 1950

K.M.   Your old headmaster, to whom we wrote explaining that you would be coming up for interview, made no mention of your French.

P.W.   No, he would not. His son scraped into Fitzwilliam House, Cambridge, and that was that. His father took some pleasure in thrashing me on the very day my mother happened to visit school to see him about some minor matter.

K.M.   Surely there would have been some vacancy for him in the Gestapo.

P.W.   Bad breath might have kept him out. He was gassed in the First World War, and we always used to say that he was still breathing it on us to make us vomit during the one class he taught: Scripture.

K.M.   Well, I'll tell you where his next vacancy is going to be: right in the gaping mouth of this waste paper bin. *(He tears the letter in half and sails it into the bin with a special smile.)* Did his son play cricket?

P.W.   No, nothing like that.

K.M.   Was he a prefect?

P.W.   Head prefect.

K.M.   So how did your prominence as a cricketer go down at school and in the village? After all, no matter how intellectual you may be, a sportsman has obligations!

P.W.   School was proud, but the local cricket club, in the village, banned me for bowling too fast at twilight.

K.M.   Lincoln has a good name for cricket. We are admired. I should tell you I too have been banned, for playing music too loudly.

P.W.   My mother's a pianist and she sometimes makes the room with the aspidistra rock. Beethoven and Co. Actually, we quite often huddle outside the door when she does a demonstration piece for a music pupil. "That's the style," she then says when they play again. They have been inspired. She is Art and my father is War. They make an interesting combination.

K.M.   Your father was in the Machine Gun Corps. A sergeant.

P.W.   Yes.

K.M.   We would be glad to have you come up to Lincoln. When did your interest in classical music begin?

P.W.   I used to dote on swing, still do, but it all began with the Hallé Concerts—Barbirolli. A group of us used to take the bus into Sheffield at weekends. I also remember Bernard Herrmann conducting the Hallé. Perhaps naturally, I preferred piano concertos, but it was there I first heard Stravinsky: *Petrouchka*. Only once, but penetrating.

Custodian, Southfield House

They has it off with themselves in their wardrobes with their mouses all red and their tongues out wobbling. Sons of the brave and the rich all right. They gets the girls in during daylight and stows them inside the walls like them casks of amontado in that American book. Comes night and they sets to work chopping wood. We heard them at it, the squeaks and shrieks, then next day the jam towels in the garbage I inspects. I always thought they come here to improve themselves from Egypt or wherever they hail from, to get some edifation. Not on your life, they comes here to stretch it and widen it, polish the knob of it while the rest of us fed on crab apples and cobweb sandwiches trains to be chimbley sweeps and Clydesdale grooms. It isn't fair with their cars and the missus ladies in furs that stink of sweat and au de cologne. Take my missus, she slaves all day but they fools her, moving the women from room to room behind her. She never sees them but she sniffs them all right, the pong of hoestrus they calls it in the surgeries, the reek of rotten blood they will always carry with them to the grave no matter how high they rise with silver silk ties and top hats to match. They look at me and see a dunce without a dunce's cap. All very well, young sirs, one of these days we are going to rise up and rummage about in your insides, just for a fry-up. And their moldy cupboards full of butter and raspberry jam, even if the ants have found it out, just like they was the advance guard of the Fifth Column. A pox on lodgers.

A COLLEGE SCOUT

Being a gentleman's gentleman implies a deference, even a servility, what with the making of beds, provision of breakfast, holding of the basin for vomit, and all such, but not always. There are precious moments when they do not call you Hobbs or Baker, but Mr. Hobbs and Mr. Baker, especially those new gentlemen of a newer class not quite certain of its social station, so they sometimes crouch under the nearest incontinent horse in hope of milder weather. Oh yes, they *la-di-da* and *Oh my!*, but they need you like the mother the midwife. You bring them out of the famous pupa into imminent adulthood, we who read more books than they and sometimes even get the big words right. Oh they come it all right, most of the time, with orders for cablegrams and a bottle of Scotch, a girl in a taxi please and some body-soiled laundry to do, but most of the time they have palace manners, and more's the pity we can't do the brainwork for them, poor sods racking their minds for a whole week and then in despair calling out for a pint of warm ale. Such is life at the top. The point is: they do not have to do well, because the doing well has been done before them, before they arrived, and they just slide into a slot for life while the likes of us watch over them. Lick stamps, wipe their bums, bath their babies, fry their eyeballs, make their beds, dump their rubbish, wipe the scum from their telephones, clean between their teeth while they sleep, and hold umbrellas over them. What you are born to, you should do it well without a sigh, like that German commissionaire who wears a big thick greatcoat and waits outside for all visitors to the hotel. Now, who was he when he's at home?

Dining Hall Scout, Lincoln

They vex me they really do, talking even while eating about the worms and blackclocks cooked up into the third boiling of the curry. I can see you would say it afterward, but not during. Protein for young gentlemen's good, not so fancy as some of your Christchurches and Magdalens where they has wedding cake in their soup and little roasted mice in their mince pies. I likes to see them quaff and trough, these young larrups, but I'd give 'em a good hiding just in case for their always nudging and choking, effing and blatting, not sconceworthy antics but just bad breeding. Their brains is in their bellies, to be sure, their bellies has no politics, oh no. The rest of us get your snap early before the rush, we just shovel it out and scrape the plates off for the fourth boiling up tomorrow. When they ran hot and cold water in this college they should have piped the soup through at the same time and pushed the dollops of rice up through the toilets. You can stand only so much until they starts slinging the stuff back at you and it makes holes in the paneling and the faces of the previous wise men hung there. The pellets could do you in if you didn't duck. O Lord, none of your *benedictus benedicats*, but instead a prayer to make the food softer even in the fourth boiling so as not to puncture et cetera and leave our stomachs in a state of relative repair.

They'll end up stopping hanging, I suppose, which deprives the condemned during her majesty's pleasure of a chance to refuse the last breakfast, the last supper, and all stations in between.

BARONESS DEIRDRE CONNAUGHT, VISITING COLLEGE

In a mood of alert bereavement she has come to inspect the space her son would have occupied had he ever come here, a scholar elect in Classics, killed in a car accident. They make a fuss of her all right, a little suspicious of her response to vacancy: the room he might have occupied, the bed, the scout, the fireplace, the quads, the famous food. It is as if, she thinks, you are the walking bereaved and you discover for the first time, so engrained are your responses to traditional acts, that someone is no longer walking alongside. You go on respecting the evacuated space beside you, fillable by none other of course, but cannot quite grasp the fact of clinical removal. Not a trace left on the atmosphere or the greensward, the slop sand or the snow. How can anyone disappear that completely? Is their entirety absolute? Are they merely lagging behind or have they gone ahead to check on a favorite buttercup? She cannot, anywhere, smell his smell, hear his phlegmy throat, feel his mushroom skin. She watches the undergrads and grads at their toil, remarking how small the boys seem, unlike certain other colleges where length seems paramount. He would have fitted in well, she thinks, being of average height and of the correct flimsy build for life among these scramblers and frolickers, who look too young to be working for degrees in this or that.

His scholarship will go to someone else, having been announced in *The Times*, and his beloved classics will find their way into what she calls the death cupboard, teeming with toys. The rough and tumble of these little squeaky boys would have suited him well; he would have liked the way they bounce off one another with glee en route for dinner. He would not have become, say, a military commander dreaming on the site of Thermopylae, or a tall rugger hero, but someone always with an appropriate tag from either language, here mourned before becoming anybody at all, his father's college, and they had put him down in the register at birth. The father cannot bear to make this funereal trip, but she has the vim for it, head held high in the veil, limousine parked outside blocking the Turl, the boy's clever ghost adaptably at home among the lawns and echoes he will always inhabit as she remembers this day of probed unfulfilment. In later years he will join that suave contingent of nominal fellows who linger and linger, licking the rims of the port glasses after the rest of High Table has gone, the specter who does not haunt.

My Mother and Mrs. Tatlow Review the Oxford Colleges

Magdalen has the river. And the deer of course. Yes. Worcester, a garden college, I gather. Balliol has the Scots brains, they say, and Jesus the Welshmen. True. When you say New College, you say *New College*, you don't say "N—." Oh yes. Queen's isn't the same as at Cambridge: only one queen. Christchurch is fashionably pronounced "*Hou*—." Oh yes. And St. Catherine's is the college with just lodgers, a cut below. Really. Keble is high church, I'm told, and of course Mansfield is clerical too. Univ, isn't that where Clement Attlee went? And the poet Shelley. Amazing. Didn't Lord Byron—No, the other. Of *course*. There's St. Edmund Hall, the smallest, properly referred to as Teddy Hall, and then there's Wadham with Mr. Bowra and Corpus Christi which it is all right to name Corpus, and then of course Brasenose, known as BNC, and Exeter, Oriel, St. John's who don't seem to attract any special mention. Oh, what about Spirochete College, my mother says, isn't there a funny word for that? Not as I'd know, she says. Isn't Paul somewhere? Lincoln, says my mother. Oh, *that*, she says. I think Jonathan is a Balliol man in the making. He will go *there*. He did.

THE DEAN OF ST. LAMPETER'S WEIGHS HIS LOT

Oh the cold, God's haughtiness turned into stuff. This is how He wants us all to feel, not only the occupants of a small college surrounding a slaughtered saint's grave. I know who he was. Can all this have been going on so early, long before our worthy selves? We are worthy, no doubt of that, but chilly, chilly, along with the mice and beetles, the spiders and the blackclocks. God's stuff, then, chiding and shrinking us at our crouch or trot. Hunched over some old manuscript or other, vaguely consecrated (ourselves) to grooming the young in God's ways, when really, truly, I would prefer to be reading for myself, free to spend time on something else, perhaps some work of renegade lewdness, were such available. They do exist, those whore books, do they not, passed from hand to hand during dinner, under the table, two-handedly, then smuggled in the folds of an academic gown to loft, garret, hovel, to the college's highest or lowest rooms. *Aula Sancti Lampetri.*

Back to the cold. Those of us who are coldest, who feel so, must surely be permitted the coarsest reading, which makes a subjective matter of the whole thing. Who is to say who is coldest? Should we be paraded out there in the quad and felt at among the gravestones? By whom? By myself, their supervisor, I the coldest of all. I was warmer before I became Dean. Chumminess made me toastier. Small college, closer huddles. Is that how it goes? In larger places, the huddles are—well, more spread out. Here, close as we are, we tend to both lose and gain heat at about the same rate. Or is that a figment? Could one of us lose more than he gains? It is just the kind of question we devote our lives to, vexing the young men's brains to make them better Christians. As I see it, you cannot lose, or gain, without being in contact with some other, unless there are certain positions—aha, *positiones!*—in which you gain more than you lose, or vice versa. Say, if the tongue were in that other's ear, but his finger in between your own thumb and forefinger. Such a person would surely win more than he would lose. He would have to, there are laws pertaining to heat exchange, although who wrote them I have no idea. Rest assured, I tell myself, there is a treatise for everything out there, suppressed but still there, ready for use. Such is one of God's providential ways, to whom all is known and thus forestalled. It is no use thinking for ourselves: we only end up doing His bidding, arcane as that may be. The best families send us their sons to be—what can it be? Made into gentlemen or believers, so we rack their brains. Set them problems about angels on the point of a hawthorn spike, and send them off again to the family seat deep in the heart of the countryside among deer and wolves. Is that all we do? Perhaps we make of them convivial fellows, convivial oafs anyway, and teach them how to eat without actually holding the food between their hands, the farm laborer's way. That's how you can tell a gentleman. He uses an implement to distance himself from what, within an hour, will become sludge in his bowels. We not only acquaint them with the point of view from the grave. We teach them about bags of excrement, always in Latin. *Colei stercoris.* The thrill of using our own language has not yet quite sunk in, but sink it will. It is one thing to parade along Logic Lane, keeping the townspeople at bay with a gorgeous spread of Latin among ourselves; it is quite another to be pretending thus to each other, so stilted, so alien. One day, I predict, talking will be as natural as eating. Would we eat in Latin or sleep in it? Some do, but I hazard that the dream is the ideal hunting ground for our own prattle. Did not Anglo-Saxon give way to our own mode of talk? There's a tumult, a shove in these things. Am I not earthier when I speak of a shove in the gut than when like some old Roman legionaire, I envision *gastric impetus* or even worse?

The day will come when even the tiny fire is obsolete and warm water, as in Ancient Rome, will course through the rooms of our colleges, even ancient piles such as this Hall, beloved but accursed: musty nest of stones and black gowns, English cheese and coarse bread. I will not see it, but I can anticipate. A new heating system will puff different curtains in different ways, and we shall be at ease in our slippers in the library, knowing we have requested that small holes be bored into our coffins beforehand, just in case, and a beloved book for the journey, filth for viaticum, say a thousand years for the journey to God, time enough to learn a treatise by heart, even a lewd one, and then perhaps another five hundred getting to know Him before getting down to the real business of salvation according to ancient precepts.

The soul, I am convinced, makes its voice heard. Long before we depart, like a bubble in a fishglue bottle, venting a tiny squeak as the pressure evens out, and there on your writing desk or your prie-dieu there comes that tiny mouse-noise of something, wanting to escape and succeeding. Like all gases. I sometimes think all we ever take in is air, and a bird flies through us avoiding the big cliffs of stodge. As after being elected Dean: you have to move from your most commodious quarters to exactly the same quarters—same narrow bed, bald water jug and basin, not even a hint of the floral on either, and the same stack of much-used scratchy blankets. No change. You are not supposed to enjoy authority any more than the life you had hitherto. Lovely word: hitherto. Come hither to what? To self-denial, as if conscripted into some static army without ever admitting your fear. Twizzle my thumbs.

So then: candles, cheese, jam, shank of lamb, slice of ham, greasy surplice, an occasional custard pie. Not much for a life of incessant pondering, the subject passed on to the young before being properly understood, so you have the half-blind leading the blind. One day it will all change, won't it? Perhaps we will all end up speaking French in here. Nothing seems certain. We could be in a jungle, sucking on stewed rhubarb. I am aghast at the arbitrariness of it all, when everything in it might have been different, but instead we dote on the way things are, as if the universe could never spawn anything else. If my days have an end, then to the end of them I can only profess an uncodified faith in the infinite, cached between a bee's knees.

CYRIL'S PAVILION

Cyril the groundsman might once have been a coach, telling the college what best to do, but his favored alternate role (he presumes) is that of dining hall scout, horny thumb stuck deep into the Windsor soup after being coated with his special chemical inferno of molasses, sawdust, ink, and parrot-do, just to keep the gentlemen on the alert for the cricket field. He will never make the grade of servant, however, his forte being how deep the spike of a boot will sink into the turf, or exactly where to pitch the ball, just short of the blind spot with the seam upright so as to gain maximum lift. He can do these things in his sleep, at least prate about them to less than enthralled audiences. No one has ever seen him play, so they have no idea of his caliber as a player. They have heard him hold forth, presumably basing all he says on a distinguished past when he was limber and able to do anything required of him. He has a spare tire now and is rumored to have modified the role of the roller that flattens out the pitch, actually harnessing prisoner girls to the shafts and having his way whoever she be in the privacy of the pavilion. It is on such escapades he really lectures, to anyone who cares to listen or to watch, his favorite phrase being "get hers

ready." He has found his niche, all right, and one can only wonder if his future will include seminars on Villiers de l'Isle-Adam with
Maurice Bowra, or even Locke, Berkeley and Hume with Dr.
Beck of Merton. He will go far, we know, but over a distance of
only inches, yearning to ruin Windsor soup day after day, but
restricted to how far a bootspike will go into human flesh if
shoved in hard. His behavior may be automatic, but he likes to
think he stops it short of being mindless.

DR. PRIVET

Behold Dr. Privet, who loves to proctor scholarship examinations (or, as he himself says with a flourish, "invigilate them"). He responds keenly to the element *vigil* embedded in the larger word. He keeps *his* vigil, back to the roaring fire that might otherwise distract the candidates and can feel the damp rising in a cloud from his woolen jacket parked too close. He adores to survey their act of frenzied writing, but almost as much he loves the words of his performance, always varying them, but usually playing favorites: "You may begin," instead of, "Start now, gentlemen," and "Please finish the sentence you are now writing," instead of, "Pens down." Always, the more elaborate terms will suit him. He was once heard to say, "Gentlemen, gently now. Would you please complete the sentence you are presently committing and deposit your script in the laundry basket at the front." He may be said to have made love to his occupation, actually wishing he might sit down with them and attempt to win an award to his own college. He'd be bound to come out tops. But he curbs himself from that, although quietly conning the examination paper, noting the stylistic fetishes of his colleagues: Stoker's passion for alliteration ("symbolist synergy"), at which he winces, or Perbethny's longing for oxymoron ("an agora of the esoteric"). They all have their little call-signs, he murmurs, and give extra credit to those who heed them. My own, I wonder if anyone ever noticed, seeing that I proctor everything in the coziness of the college, would be a question about Carlyle that always includes the word "froth." Keeper of the gate, he will proctor or invigilate in his grave, tugging young winners down to his decay, just to keep an eye on them and save them from cheating, which would be odd indeed since the question papers are opportunistic and recklessly individual.

Privet keeps an eye on all.

In the afterlife it will not be as bright as in that college classroom, and we shall be obliged to go on writing with no hope of being published, rewarded, or patted on the back. There will be no fires, but the most virtuous of all of us will be permitted to watch extermination-camp horrors on a screen that reflects filled bookcases behind them, so giving to the experience a touch of studious amenity: bookshelves superimposed upon butchers. The place's motto, filched from the Boy Scouts, reads *Be Prepared*.

7

AMATEURS

A Mellifluous Beehive

You did not have to be around Oxford very long, especially its literary circles, to run into the assorted plays of David Lutyens, who seemed prolific with plenty of money behind him. He came, I learned, from a distinguished, nay a revered family of artistic gifts, and the foreign flavor of the name added luster to his work. I never got much from his plays, which struck me as close to fustian, but they were being performed, my only problem with that being that I was a movie fan and could be found staring for the third time at *Rome, Open City* or *Bitter Rice* before I showed up at any play. I was one of those benighted fellows who preferred to *read* his Shakespeare.

Even then, while most of us were finding our way among the tenements and palaces of literature, Lutyens, as well as creatively pondering the dramatic potential of a Judas Iscariot, was reflecting on the piety and Christian mystagogy to be found in the plays of Christopher Fry and Paul Claudel, the burden of which he published abroad in *The Tulane Drama Review*. His own poems appeared in English journals and such distant ones as *The Beloit Poetry Journal*. Indeed, his concern with American writing showed up in the critical book he was writing, *The Creative Encounter*, which dealt with Hart Crane, Robinson Jeffers, Robert Lowell, Archibald MacLeish, and other American poets. He was not so much hiding his light under a bushel as hiding a bushel under his light, in comfortable secrecy plotting ambitious volumes we knew nothing about. His interest in European and American literature singled him out when, perhaps, what he really wanted was to be accepted by the *Isis* clique. In that sense, he suffered an Oxford fate.

And then he suffered another one. Trying all manner of means to locate and seek further into his career, I wrote to his former London publishers whose name had figured so largely on his books, but got no answer. He had fallen out of sight, by the wayside. I hadn't thought his work that great, but he was worth remembering, hauled from behind the portcullises or sentry-boxes of history—just for having lived, for having been *there*, for having made his ripple, without which the universe would have been slightly different.

Lutyens, hailed or ignored, was in evidence, but so was Dita Pevsner, son of an architect, along with a dozen more. Everyone you met had some fancy, potent family tree, and I sometimes wondered what would happen if I passed myself off as the missing link from the Sitwell family. The village was rife with rumor about just such a possibility, in the abstract of course (no names, no pack-drill), but gossip-designed and full of Midlands flavor. Many a slip, it was murmured at Billy Cooper's draper's shop, between cup and lip, heavily implying backstairs malarkey best spotted in the retinue strolling down the village street, past the tripe shop in whose window the cricket team for Saturdays was posted. But who, *by* whom? Neither Dame Edith nor Sir Osbert were likely candidates, anyway. Sacheverell then? It made little sense, so the mischief probably belonged in a previous generation. In any case, I told myself I was that teratological gremlin the self-made boy. I had a degree and would soon have a "book."

Such grandiosity. Wiser now, yet perhaps not better informed, I would have called it a chap-book; and, in a wild moment, perhaps wondered if a chap-book can ever become a dick-flick.

That "book" would appear with work by, among others, Elizabeth Jennings, Pearce Young, James Price, Donald Hall, Simon Broadbent, Peter Dale Scott, and George Steiner. Ninepenny pamphlets, these, no more than that, with a perfunctory bio on the back (*I* was "writing an allegorical novel on various aspects of contemporary life," God help me), and edited by Michael Shanks and Oscar Mellor, published at Swinford, Eynsham, Oxon by Shanks and Mellor for The Fantasy Press, and, wondrous to relate, reviewed in the warmest terms by the *Times Literary Supplement*—for most of us our first review. The pamphlets are worth money nowadays, representing as they did the newest and most privileged poetry being written: a sowing of the field, I thought, mostly for people who were going to continue as poets whereas I would back away into loose baggy fiction with an interlude for painting (I did collages, in the main, on mostly political themes). The old gang, someone said, but a rarer gang than populated the annual volumes of *Poetry from Oxford* and *Oxford Poetry*, in which that much bigger gang aired its wares and committed to eternity names otherwise forgotten. At Oxford, there was always print, from broadside to vanity volume, and it was hard to keep up; I never did find out what became of Geoffrey Bush's stories, he being the only one of us attempting serious fiction at the time (he the son of the scholar Douglas). Oxford was a mellifluous beehive, a whirligig of amateur fascinations, and at times it was hard to believe that many of us were going nowhere at all. The workaday world would gobble us up and spit us out.

People one had just missed were already, one heard, making waves in London, and at times it looked simpler just to ride the train and take on London proper. Oxford seemed like a military training school for young cadets who, going through martial motions, imagined themselves soldiers of lethal heft and sublime posture, where of course both it, and the beloved Oxford we inherited, had more than a touch of the nursery. How tough was the outside world going to be? Our Americans said it would be brutal, getting started and set up. Oh no, we said, with Oxford stamped on us we could do no wrong; we were the elect and the desired, although not far away, under the aegis of science and clarity, there was another species of graduate from Cambridge, as well as the horde from redbrick universities all descending on London like the wolf on the fold. There is no doubt we expected to be babied and cosseted, just for having

climbed to the top of the heap *in statu pupillari* or while teething.
Was our work that good? Some of it was, and the proud possessor
of a Fantasy Press pamphlet reviewed favorably in the *TLS* could
walk on air. There was almost no need to try for anything ever
again. I wonder if the winners of prizes and the authors of pamphlets
at American universities feel that close to New York publishing; I
doubt it. The truth seemed to be that Oxford, not Cambridge
(too far away), was a satellite of London. After all, John Lehmann
and C. Day Lewis came to talk to us and check us out, although they
went to Cambridge too where the American John Berryman would
roost, and ogle the girls.

Actually, there was a great deal of work going on, not published
because not showable, but serious work done by greenhorns who had
just had a glimpse of their own majesty and were chicken about
parading it too soon. I do think some of the American poets among
us shot on ahead, blooded in a more demanding ethos, reflecting
early, to our envy, a richer turmoil than ours. We sensed something
brasher, more savage, at work. We were clever, all right, but somehow spun by too many catchy tunes. Eyeing Edwin Muir and
George Barker, say, rather than the so-called Welsh Apocalyptic
Henry Treece or the genuine surrealist David Gascoyne, we were just
shopping around, whereas the Americans among us appeared to have
decided which school they wanted to belong to, which mode of verse
suited them best. In other words, we were less professional than they,
more smart-mouthed amateurs than anything else, whereas they had

schemes and agenda, not necessarily right, but laid out, virtually final, even consecrated to a certain progenitor. I became interested in the very concept of the amateur, who felt a certain disinclination to join, be committed, give up one thing so as to have another. This is not to say that the lax, loose-wristed amateur (Isaiah Berlin's fox to the complementary hedgehog) would not come up eventually with solid, gifted work; but the introit, the ramp, was trickier, squeakier; you allowed yourself more time to make mistakes and shop around. This must explain itself as the difference between American gogetterdom and English casualness—until some appalling crisis like the Battle of Britain shows up, and then the English take life seriously, even if they settle down again with staggering indifference (in 2001 part of the RAF, which slaughtered air Nazis in the skies of southern England, was for sale to Germany!). If this is not amateurism, one wonders what is.

Well, we were trying our paces in the early Fifties, not so much heavily committed as creatively pregnant, as charmed by being social as by what others of us wrote. There was no problem in getting into print; indeed, the problem may have been keeping out of it to stew on things rather more. There was no doubt that, whatever fuddy-duds inhabited Oxford curricula, the social side of the university was unceasing, and one's mantelpiece was crammed with ornate cards inviting, inviting, inviting. The university was too receptive for our own damned good, I suppose, but how can the dancer appraise the dance? It was a champagne cotillion.

Was there snobbery? My parents, and others, always asked me this about Oxford and all I could ever say was that, wherever I had been, I had never witnessed any, not in college, at games in the Parks, in the university at large, or even in All Souls. Not everyone who fancied himself or herself top rung was, but who cared? We had risen like sap and were one another's accomplices. We applied our social good graces to one another like ointment. As for myself, coming from one of the least heeded grammar schools in the land, and perhaps in the early stages feeling a bit like a fugitive from the movie *The Corn is Green* (clever boy from Welsh mining town gets to Oxford with help of Bette Davis! Imagine such a plot in real life!), I never looked back. Indeed, as my father with some bitterness pointed out, it was easier to get into Oxford than to buy suitable clothes for the local grammar school, and he wished he'd had a go at the one place instead of the other. The only easier place, he said, was the Army, who provided you with bed and board, kit and caboodle. Everything. Sparrow would have agreed with him; both had a rather rosy view, not shared by me, of the jovial companionship to be found in the ranks. I only heard that tone in my father once again, when for a broken ankle in the RAF I got a pension larger than he did for his dead eye. "*Officers*," he said. "I'm just as glad you're an Oxford man." Yes, he would have read modern history of course with a special subject in trench warfare, but also in his first assignment as a Black and Tan in Ireland, during those endless troubles pronounced, "Thrubbles."

HANDWORK

Ingenious as I can be with my hands, especially in carpentry, I can never hope to surpass my father's manual dexterity, covering as he did a wide range of engineering and technical innovations, for which he would wander away and return with some little gadget specially conjured up for the occasion. These he called widgets. To witness a problem was, for him, to recognize instantly the remedy, so much so that his non-existent workbench was his spectrum. The wide world always contained the makings, metal or wood or bakelite, and the idea sprang at once to his mind. Many's the time we have sat, before us on the table a huge box holding the dismembered pieces of a nominal seaplane, putting together from that panoply of wings, floats, fuselages and propellers some as yet undevised model, sometimes he and I constructing a different version. He would need a float I had already seized, and vice versa. We really needed two kits, an eventuality the maker's boast ignored, but somehow we compromised, and our pretty seaplanes emerged, his and mine, modified at the last minute as they often had to be. What a gorgeous present for a boy. I also had a miniature lathe, a "Juneero," tendentious neologism that it was, and sundry

boxes of erector sets called Meccano. In the long run, as the original cardboard boxes fell apart, all these apparently incompatible
components ended up in the same huge reinforced box, both
chamber of horrors and Ali Baba's cave. Seaplanes came first, but
we also made cranes, cars, bridges, and other kinds of planes, even
a simulated aero-engine we supplemented with a little electric
motor bought for a birthday.

Here was the source of the son's ability to invent and build, all
with somewhat battered and scarred hands of course. It was what
origami experts might call handwork, not handiwork. Hours and
days slipped by as we constructed together to the sounds of my
mother's piano, mainly Beethoven and Bach: an idyll of a boyhood
well spent, but also a prophecy of the son's ability to fold paper
gliders, make models of just about any World War II airplane, and
useful fretwork things to be distributed around the house. Our
house was an amateur Bauhaus. Creativity was its very name, as
my mother so often proved after dispatching her last music pupil
and then playing the masterworks correctly for us who remained.
That was how to do it, she implied, and the worse the tiros
played the more triumphant her definitive version would become.

"I need another float," he says, "can't have a lopsided seaplane
can we? A sponson is it?"

I unscrew one of my own floats and hand it to him: water in the
desert. "Too little," he says. "I don't care for these little shrimpy
things."

He notices I have attached my own floats too far back; the plane will stagger and stall. I tell him.

"Not if you unscrew the floats and struts. Now, if you were a handy workman, you'd have drawn plans first, and you'd have calculated the angles required." He says *calclated*.

So, we are going to stall as soon as we lift off the mirror of Lake Windermere. I am quite willing to have my umpteenth model be a freak; I have French poetry to go back to, and Sartre on Baudelaire and Tintoretto, but the old aviation-lure haunts me still.

"Wake up," my father says. "You'll never catch up at this rate. I'll have a hangar full of planes before you even twig what's going on."

"And you'd have taken all the pieces," I say. "You do help yourself to my toys."

Notice my emphasis on hands, nimble and busy. I draw a straight line from those days to my rather Luddite performance with paper and scissors, Elmer's glue and wood whittled to exactly the right shape. A typescript correction entails, for me, a retyped slip of paper, tailored to the exact dimensions of the text, and then glued in place, making everything a palimpsest about which ("pasteups") you have to warn the xerox people. That habit, written up elsewhere, is just one example, machine-defying and retrograde, but also eloquent about the glory of handwork, not essentially different from computerized corrections, but closer to the illuminated manuscripts of medieval monks. It has to do with time as well as hands, I suspect. To work thus is to abolish *durée*, and to reduce complexity to simple terms, maybe the simplest, so that I can be found scrawling on yellow tablets with pen and ink or 2B pencils, actually coloring certain parts of the manuscript with water-soluble tints, and generally making of an innocent and somewhat homogeneous document a thing not so much of beauty as of surprise. Perhaps a touch of pre-Raphaelite William Morris from Exeter, the college next door, guilelessly invades my conception of subverted origami. I am intent on gussying things up, not on making them look efficient or machine-made. Some assiduous researcher, hell-bent on the truth, could spend a lifetime peeling off my correction slips, easing them off more or less intact to expose the first thought, the word I chose against in the crescendo of composition. Not worth it of course, but you never know what attracts the assiduous researcher on a rainy day.

The main idea is to transform the written text into something else *as well*, to make it appeal on another level. When some devout researcher finds in my novels a piece of action or a message inscribed on a paper airplane that will fly pilotless to Australia and back, he/she will have found a trace of my boyhood's amateur leanings. That must be why I take my time, countering a tendency to write quickly. I revise at snail's pace, ever looking aside at drawings and photos, objects and maps, none of these enfolded into the manuscript, but spiritually on the premises. I suppose that, even with my series of electric typewriters and correction tapes on hand for

when I get impatient, I am fixated on the toil of the artisan, much
as Churchill was on bricklaying—maybe a sop to the unexpended
energy that's part and parcel of the compositional act. I'm not sure,
but this is surely why I responded so favorably to the pamphlets of
the Fantasy Press, all done by hand with God's or Darwin's own
slowness, and then (some of them) numbered and signed. Heaven
help those with carpal tunnel trouble, unable to sign their handwork, for that is part of the signal act. In my time, to get things
right, I have manufactured cardboard models of the OK Corral,
revealing the gunslingers' respective fields of fire, and of course a
working model of the mutilated Colonel von Stauffenberg, mainly
to see how he looked with his briefcase bomb, and how much he
could see with his one eye (like my father, who had no depth perception and not much inkling sideways). Such forays come naturally to me, obviating the purchase and use of complex electronics,
and enabling me to function in my primitive way almost anywhere.
No creative act was more mobile than mine, I guess, my mind
somehow always on my father's keen historical purview of the
trenches, courtesy of his maps and flags and the footnotes to Sir
John Hamerton's history of the war.

My desk is a mess, but I have at least made a concession to tidi-
ness by retwisting trombone paper clips (as Latin-Americans call
them) to hang on the rim of an empty Roma jar, so that on the
hooks that lean out I can suspend scissors, nail scissors, other
paperclips, and anything else that can dangle. The same fidget as

built those planes is at work here, I suspect, and behind all of this there is a loving slowness, a medieval crawl that counterpoints the seeming speed of my imagination. There is more to it, though, from a completely different zone: I can sometimes pretend I am doing brain surgery on my own text, manipulating tiny slips of paper into position in the exact place needed, with the new word printed thereon, breath held, not a tweezer in sight, the paper slip held by its edges so as not to mar the thin coat of glue applied then wiped off. These antics might distress someone who works at a computer and corrects in a trice, but I have some ancient, atavistic sense of a text's intactness, its holiness, thinking its final version deserves its full creative history, the accumulated palimpsest, say, executed preferably on thick paper on its way to cardboard. So my manuscripts tend to bulk large, at least the ribbon copy does, smudges and Elmer stains and ill-aligned correction slips included. Perhaps my handling of Walter Pater's calling-card sized slips persuaded me long ago, and I never got over my initial recognition of a manuscript page as composed from a hundred vying components glorious in their independence but celestial in combination.

So I have no e-mail, no floppy disks, but heaps of rubber-banded first drafts or securer wads tied with string or cord. I do own a fax, which I regard as magic, but that along with an electric typewriter is the limit of my prowess, and requests for digital versions, or even scanned ones, go unheeded. I hardly know the lingo. I discovered these tendencies when at Oxford and beginning to write, sharply aware of the devout act I was addressing myself to: ink, paper, blotter (in those days), gum arabic, carbon paper, correction slips, correction fluid (surely not some seepage from the jails), and stony-hard erasers mounted in the tips of typewriter brushes. I was a committed scribe.

And why not? I had to make up for lost time, having at school been judged by the teachers too dense for Latin, too barbaric for Art, and thus relegated to Shop. I entered Oxford as a fully qualified carpenter with a flair for mechanical drawing. I smiled when I at last was allowed to mess with Latin (Art never), and discovered that not one of my fellow pupils knew how to make a letter rack or draw the cross-section of an airplane engine.

GEEZER STUFF

To this theme of my parents watching over my progress or lack of it in foreign places, I would like to return, rather in the mood of one Virginia-and-Kimmi, sisters perhaps or mother and daughter, who on a mostly completed jigsaw on a Florida hotel mezzanine left the following postcard: "Dear Maids, children, and puzzlers, Feel free to puzzle, but don't take the puzzle apart!" This mood, like someone carrying a full glass of water and fretting about spilling the meniscus, is a moving one and no doubt has cosmic implications. It was clear to my mother that I would be unable to follow her into the Royal Academy of Music, anyway, and to my father that I had no talent as a machine-gunner (though adequate to make repairs)—he did, however, sometimes reminisce about the bogus order that stationed him, quite alone with his Vickers, on the Belgian coast expecting an enemy attack from the western flank. We would have been all right, he said, fighting them off until help arrived. I always wondered about that, but he never.

Instead, I want to examine the notion of the amateur, who does his thing for love of it, much as I, in another domain, played cricket for the love of it, merely being paid for my traveling

expenses: county, university, club, village cricket, any kind of it
because of the lure and the thrill. My uncle Douglas, that superb
batsman, had been much the same, and he remained always an
object of love and reverence in the family, bowled out by pneumonia in South Africa before he was thirty. With him on one
voyage home, he had brought his collection of African butterflies,
each one big as a hand, and eventually I inherited these, playing
with them, nudging and posing them on maps of Africa much as
I supposed he himself had during the chilly evenings that killed him,
outside on the terrace in an open-necked shirt.

An old writing student of mine wrote to say she'd gone on to
the University of Chicago to take an M.A. in thirteenth-century
Italian poetry. Now *there* was an ideal introit to the roiling,
brawling twentieth century, as apt to stir the literary juices as any
ancient war. My feeling was that those who pursued classical literature, history and thought, had had their heads turned backward
to enormous profit. It sounds incongruous, but it brought to
mind, even for me the newcomer to Latin, some worthy old tags:
exquirite antiquam matrem, seek out the ancient mother. Such,
I always presumed, was the philosophy behind the training of future
prime ministers on what disrespectful persons called "geezer stuff."
They read it, I hope, because they loved it, believing as I myself did
that humanity was much the same wherever you sliced it, and the
oldest cut, with all its thinking arranged around it complete, was
the stablest introduction to a human society in the round. I loved

the idea that nobody was adding to the corpus of the works, so that you could make a statement about it (say masochism in the love poetry if you will forgive the anachronism) without fear of contradiction except from those who had misread the texts. There was more too, involving the canny drift of the political mind discernible in such authors as Tacitus, Sallust, Pliny the Elder, Caesar, even Herodotus. I had my own favorites, most of them "decadents" such as Catullus and Ovid, Suetonius and Tibullus, but I revelled in Virgil and had actually read two books of *The Odyssey* in Greek—small beer for Oxford, but I had at least shown willing, like the Nick Nolte colonel in *The Thin Red Line*, the movie, who spouts during the battle for Guadalcanal the Greek taught him at West Point: "*rosy-fingered dawn.*" And this to a *Greek* subaltern at that! It is not the craving to drop classical tags that animates me, it is the vision of a world so thoroughly fathomed that it can be summed up concisely for initiates, who of course already know it all and merely rejoice at the repeated sound of what they love.

This is an unusual thing. I was at Oxford, by the grace of God and Edith Sitwell, say, and here I was reading all the wrong books, the unprescribed ones, nonetheless soaking up second by second Oxford's ineffable gift, without which you are Not Even Human (which was how I dubbed NEH: National Endowment for the Humanities), part of a friend's visiting title. In a word, I was open to the grand seepages of literature, untidily, but vouchsafed a view of the main in all its cranky glory. I was no doubt slow to appreciate this view, but I knew all right that, for four luxuriant years, something jubilant and lavish was going on, equipping me as I had never thought anyone could be equipped at an early age, not in Sparrow's beloved epitaphs (the faint funereal fimbriations of Latin-lovers' last gasps), but the foundation of all letters that had sent Dryden and Pope into the world of translation, and even the pastel soul of Gilbert Murray. It was not that I did not find some Greek thin and passive, or the imagery of their tragedies a bit wan, or that Tibullus isn't a bit of a grinder and Caesar a bit of a Patton. It is that, assimilated into the round, as at least one Oxford program devised it, this was the way to flex your muscles in the presence of giants. Why not? Even as I was in my harum-scarum way attempting it, there was a profit to be taken: something mellow and insidious, as the French intend when speaking of sunbathing as an attempt to *profiter du soleil.* You sunbathe amid the Greeks, you get sensual among the Romans. You get ready for Mallarmé and Rimbaud, if I may be so bold and off-limits.

So was it for this amateurism that Sparrow the classical scholar had taken me on as no one ever before in all his history as a don, and Wilson of the English Faculty, over whose ornate mahogany desk I had upset a full open bottle of violet Stephens ink during my first interview (I was nervous)? In truth I was something of a dabbler, a hanger-on in fortunate places relying always on what some old comedy had uncouthly described as "elp from a unexpected quar'er." Muscular stripling, with a lovely degree in English behind him, I wanted to branch out, and had, and would, playing Autolycus as I snapped up all manner of unconsidered trifles: Rilke, Homer, Bernanos, Malraux. I was not going to cross the channel like a shuttle service with my fellow collegians Ernest Hofer and his manicured mannered drawl, or Len Polonski with his suburban twang, but I was up to the same kind of thing: trespassing by going away, ever hoping for a miracle, which came many years later in Paris when, unannounced, I popped in to the Village Voice Bookshop and found my portrait staring down at me from the top of a broad pillar. *Res ipse loquitur.* The thing speaks for itself. Well, it spoke, anyway. That is how you know that your immersion in the "wrong" culture has paid off. Or when René Char sends you a new edition inscribed "en bien cordial hommage."

I anticipate, grateful to have met one friend, not an Oxford man but a Cornell man, who knows much more about literature than I do, who only the other day, learning I'd just been consulted by a Bulgarian lady who was writing in German because the Bulgarian literary tradition was feeble, cited my friend Claudio Magris's *Danube*, and the pages therein devoted to that same Bulgarian literature. Clearly she had not read them. *I* had, though, having written the only review that Magris's marvelous book had received in the United States. Such are the epiphanies of dogged flirtation.

Speaking of flirtation, my almost constant girl friend of this period, Puffin Blain, who graduated in English before joining

BOAC as a stewardess (as she was then called), had developed a theory about the agitated mobility of men's rear ends, the theory stating that the more scurrying, wobbling motion the rear end displayed, the brighter so to speak was the occupant. It had to be a small rear end. I thought an itchy prostate explained all, and said so, but she was adamant, and *I* did not qualify, having a muscular bowler's back and an abnormally savage cutting action from raised arm to delivery of the ball. Sturdy rear that put weight behind the arm. I vowed to twitch more when walking away, but I wasn't built for it.

I wondered if she worked for a less cosmopolitan airline and saw a different kind of rear end waddling down the aisle, she would change her views: Air South West, say, or Air Mexico. Something such. I still could not see the link between brain ability and bum motility, though I knew of links between the fourth finger and the yawn, between inverted nipples and migraine, even between deviated septum and atrial fibrillation, but my *materia medica contorta* didn't go far enough for the quick bum and the frisky brain. It was a yarn cooked up by Chaz, a bored pilot (with hyperactive small buttocks, of course) and would only get her into trouble. She spent much of her time on the India run and was probably half-Hindu already. She now traded in a kind of cockahoop jocosity designed to lead you astray. From an altogether more serious point of view, I told her that he who bites the bullet need not eat the gun.

8

HEROICS

Pluck

Let me come back to snobbery for a moment, at least to a variety of it that is only incidentally so. It's nothing to do with intellect or social standing. In the movie *The Dam Busters*, that classic of superhuman (yet wasteful) valor, in which the Royal Air Force bombs several dams in the Ruhr with huge losses, there is a sense both early on and late in which the cream of the cream has been assembled at one base to form a special squadron. Wing Commander Guy Gibson arrives at Scampton to take charge of "Squadron X" and finds, already there, some of his favorite veterans: Australians and New Zealanders, and the Cambridge Californian "Dinghy" Young, who has already been shot down twice into the English Channel and made it back home in his rubber dinghy. At movie's end we see Young's room, with on the wall a scroll commemorating some Oxford-Cambridge athletics meet, on which appears the following legend: "2 H. M. Young (Trinity)." Clearly he came in second for Cambridge. The colleges listed for the other two competitors, third and fourth respectively, assign them to "Magd," which must stand for Magdalene, the Cambridge one whereas the Oxford one is Magdalen. An Oxford man was clearly the winner, and this is a Cambridge scroll, property of the now dead or missing Dinghy Young, who this time has no rubber boat to save him.

We learn that Young was a hefty, calm man able to swallow a pint of beer without drawing a single breath. He is the senior flight commander, already chosen by Guy Gibson. But wait: one of the other two flight commanders is Henry Maudslay, an Oxford rowing Blue, in whose room we see an amputated commemorative oarblade undecipherably hung on a wall. Maudslay, suave and discreet, is a graduate too of the Oxford University Air Squadron, not a boozer at all, but a man of stable repute. Also killed in the attack on the dams.

Add to this company Joe McCarthy from Brooklyn, once a lifeguard at Coney Island, huge and blue-eyed, who has joined the RAF as a volunteer. These are Gibson's tough guys: athlete, oarsman, champion swimmer; not just tough, but men of proven and conspicuous honor. Would Gibson have picked football players? Rugger players, yes, and cricketers perhaps: both habituated to taking pain and persisting all the same, suggesting here the presence of a dedicated elite well-endowed with what the Royal Air Force calls "officer qualities" or OQs. Gibson wanted, from the Commonwealth and the USA, but also from Oxbridge, those with the guts to endure impossible pain, spiritual agony, and death. He chose others too, but this was the core of his squadron, embodying some of the brave, dogged heart that typified the Oxford martyrs of long ago.

I have often wondered about the overlap of masochism with spiritual nobility, the assumption that, when the game is up, we have to look to the cream of the cream, in whom presumably the stiff upper lip accompanies an inerasable sense of honor. Does pain ennoble? Not necessarily. Does privilege exalt? Not always or even often. So the notion of an Oxbridge supremacy in leadership merits a closer look, demanding attention to the role of amateurism in suffering (Archbishop Cranmer, for example, may be said to have been an amateur at shoving one hand, first, into the fire that consumed him in 1556 in Oxford, whether or not he resorted to the hair shirt). He had never practiced doing any such thing, although his obtuse feat recalls for us the burning match of T. E. Lawrence who claimed the trick is not to mind. The line fits Cranmer just as well, suggesting that, behind the paradigms of heroism, there is a desperate aloofness that bypasses a pain beyond all understanding, and indeed welcomes it for show, drama, from some yearning to cut a final figure or at least undergo an unblemished ordeal in the midst of plurality's froth. A contained selflessness flickers in the penumbra of ghastly immolations, and perhaps the Oxford-Cambridge Boat Race, or the Cross, are the ideal training-grounds. Is this what draws outsiders to the mystique of the Boat Race, because it toughens them too? Other Oxbridge duels excite very few. There seems to be an under-mythology of the half-blues who ignore the other sports at which the twin universities compete (or competed). I do recall another facet of snobism, now defunct, that pitted both universities at cricket against the first-class counties, and a miserable job Oxford and Cambridge usually made of it. Such was a grace and favor encounter denied all other campuses; Oxford versus a first-class county was not something to be much admired: only rowers, runners, swimmers, as Wing Commander Gibson proved. Many of those real-life men did not come back from this famous mission, but it had been assumed that they would all be capable of making the supreme sacrifice way beyond the habitual aches and pains of an athletic career.

I do not think that persuasion has quite died. A rower remains supreme, perhaps because of *The Dam Busters* in real life. The rowers are famous for being famous, and I think many ex-rowers, certainly of the Oxford and Cambridge variety, have advanced to positions of authority and power predicated on a toughness no longer flexed. I myself never took the slightest interest in rowing, and never will, conveniently remembering that at least 150 top cricketers have committed suicide: an appalling number easily exceeding the suicide figures for other sports, one explanation, provided by a former England cricket captain who took a first and became a shrink, being that at least the batter has long periods of the match to sit indoors, aloof, especially if he gets out a lot and his big day lasts only seconds. Perhaps the slow attritional nature of the game explains so high a suicide rate, but as a bowler I often felt I was out on the field too much, toiling and perspiring, and I would have loved a respite in the cool of the pavilion, soft drink in hand, my next sleep eloquent on my shoulder.

A snobism of journalistic allusion attends the names of colleges, so that the best-known ones are Balliol, Christchurch, Magdalen, and so forth, stripped of the word "college," and the same applies to the Trinity and King's of Cambridge. You may read about Balliol unsuffixed or see such a reference as "a Balliol man," but you never see mention of "a Worcester College man," and so forth. These are tiny holdovers from another, gilded age, the brand names of unarguable perfection, at least in the popular mind, and I think the cult and the name-dropping has died out with co-educational colleges, which is just as well. Needless to say, nobody even now refers to other universities and their caliber in such facile sobriquets because, I guess, nobody thinks about them. Oxford and Cambridge have been there forever, and that is that. The vicarious fan seems a houseproud hypochondriac.

Is there, I wonder, a Cambridge version of the old saying "You can always tell an Oxford man, but you can't tell him much." A simple substitution of university name would work the trick, but I have never heard it, and the phantom paragon that is Oxford continues to rule the roost. At a reading in New York, a man came up to me afterwards and said the one word "Wadham" to indicate his college. As he saw it, shaking my hand, no other words were necessary, and I suppose the extreme end of such assumption is quite wordless with Oxford men and women capable of recognizing one

another without effort. Indeed, to go even farther, a Balliol man
should be able to spot a Somerville lady. I foresee years of intricate
and joyful wordlessness while the rest of the world's graduates go
floundering on. If snobism there be, I find it a promise of pan-
tomime, long denied you, but at last leaking into the open like a virus
just to tell everyone else they don't belong. Funny Evelyn Waugh-like
novels have a field day with such haughty clubism, and that is no
doubt the best destiny for the snooty stuff. One's Oxford days
remain indelible as perhaps the most emancipated of one's life, so no
wonder a Pavlovian twitch dogs the prestigious name and opens
doors to wonderlands long lost. As who should say, if God had not
founded Oxford, we should have been obliged to invent it, as Q. D.
("Queenie") Leavis, wife to the critic F. R., did in a 1935 *Scrutiny*
essay when citing "the feminine charm of Oxford."

Discussants within these two old universities find better matters to talk about, scanting the collision of the two boats during a
recent race to make the point that, at least as far as first-class
degrees are concerned, Cambridge inflates its numbers by including firsts taken in the first part of the Tripos, while Oxford cites only
firsts awarded on finals—a huge difference and utterly misleading.
"Oxford is slipping" goes the litany, but it's only a mathematical
illusion, and it would be wiser not to talk about these things at all.
Such prattle is easy meat for heads of colleges, like complaints that
the examiners have not singled out a college's geniuses, once
again, and you become aware, if you care at all, that the university

system and the college system are often at odds even though in teaching and lecturing they overlap. I suppose athletics is a suitable alternative to worry about, in many instances not branding someone for life with an inferior degree (or, indeed, vastly exaggerating their abilities). Getting the degree is hard enough work, and the melodramas attending its *ad hominem* rituals occupy too much valuable time. Yet Oxford people of whatever stamp tend to do better in life than nonpareils from elsewhere (except in the world of high finance), and the cachet remains worthwhile.

SWANK

At the hands of the presumably envious, a dying breed, Oxford's good name gets a bad press, as when, in an episode of *Law and Order*, cop classic replete with legal jargon and skinny women, a suave, slightly obese Nigerian chief masquerading as a diplomat explains to the police that he learned to smoke during his days at Oxford. Clearly, back in his native land he is going to hang. He is what they used to call (not on TV) a bounder, a rascal, a scoundrel, and his somewhat overweight body tautly togged in the British manner warns you that he has acquired other foreign ways as well and is not to be trusted, especially with diplomatic plates. Whenever such gonifs appear on TV, intoning the brand name, they damn themselves instantly, because they have either soared beyond their station or can't think of anything else to say. Their job, the implication seems to be, is to be grateful for a good education and shut up about it, certainly not parading it like a dip in the fountain of youth. Oxbridge will soon enough emerge, they say; one need not rehearse one's good reception. I am impressed by the number of usually black criminals who appear in various TV series, having been to Oxford or Harvard and having remained unhinged ever since. What's being said?

Thanks to movie stars, the word "swank" is likelier to be heard as a surname than as the noun it used to be in my childhood, when it meant "show-off." A "swankpot" was precisely that, and I suspect that enthusiasts of the dark or light blue on the river profess a lifelong, upwardly mobile membership, not so much architectural or colorbound as vaguely social. Wholly unconnected fans claim to be Oxford or Cambridge supporters and cheer as if their lives depend upon it. I suppose fans of Manchester United, say, or like a nephew of mine who is a Barnsley football fan, have a no more substantial link. It's a matter of idle fancy or, indeed, as with certain players, pop marketing. Perhaps the star player has a modish wife or one who happens to be a known singer. According to Desmond Morris, whose early pre-Oxford paintings I used to publish, there are football tribes, and by the same token there must be boat race tribes as well. I then begin to wonder about the connotations of dark and light blue. There must be social rather than astute discriminations between the university of Newton and the university of Oscar Wilde, say, between the staid strictness of the one that has the Cavendish Laboratory in its midst and the one with an art atelier. In other words, Oxford remains the haunt of prime ministers and has a *réclame* always denied the other place. If Oxford is cheese, Cambridge is cheeses, or so the popular claquerie might think, somehow conjuring out of thin air the kind of person who has Oxford tendencies versus the one who goes the other way. There may be logic in it for people who like Cecil

Rhodes or his memory, for there are no Rhodes Scholars at Cambridge and no "name" scholarships of comparable repute. In the RAF, soon after Oxford, I was part of a special unit in which the most Oxford-like chap came from the University of Exeter, and it was the Cambridge historian who attributed his trips to the toilet to a certain "quickening" within, which in its self-indulgent, ostentatious way might have seemed more Oxonian than anything. The Oxonians were on the whole rather quiet and touchy, each capable of flamboyance and exaggeration, one an insane driver who aimed at local peasants, one who ran his entire life around boxer dogs, and one whose prose had a distinctly purple or fruity look.

Maybe there's something in it, in the distinctions I made earlier, as they crept upon me in spite of all logic. Could it be that Oxford people are crankier, more self-indulgent and self-important, more swankpots than Cambridge show-offs? It is hard to know, but perhaps supporters of the dark blue have assumed such characteristics, somehow identifying dark blue (much as big business psychologists do) as the color of wealth, reticence, and stability whereas its lighter counterpart is flightier and erratic. The remarkable thing is the fervor of the otherwise uninvolved, making one wonder at the whimsical eclecticism of spectators. I do believe that, during the days of Mrs. Thatcher, former Prime Minister, there were those who went Oxford because of her and those who dropped Oxford for the same reasons. Your affiliation changes, presumably, according to the personifications of the day. Early on, in my salad days, I got an object lesson in varsity preference after charming interviews with a Cambridge historian in Sidney Sussex College, the college of Oliver Cromwell, and a Yeats critic of renown in Selwyn College (where I almost went), and a look into Milton's narrow bedroom in Christ's, where he was known as the Lady of Christ's. Yet I went dark blue for unfathomable reasons, swapping colleges like a cardsharp, perhaps divining that the Oxford attitude to literature was more Paterian than clinical Cambridge. How wrong I was. The Oxford attitude was staid and stodgy, and Cambridge's clinical, almost New Critical approach made sage points about the details of texts. *Quel* mess. In the end, I think I plumped for Oxford for quasi-social reasons because it was a wisp more famous than Cambridge, and the varsity-fancying game had become a bore.

I had certainly no desire in after-years to attribute my cigarette-smoking to Oxford days, like some Nigerian swell. In my day, you flaunted the college of your choice with a warm striped scarf, a custom I think has rather gone out nowadays; this is the era of the T-shirt, after all, but I still have my dark blue and light blue striped Lincoln scarf (now *there*'s hedging for you!), which, folded across my thorax in a St. Andrew's diagonal cross, keeps out the winter wind when I find myself in the wrong climate. My old Lincoln ties have gone, as well as the blazers of cricket, the emblem ties for prowess, whereas the gaudiest ties have survived, like the Bermuda one, screaming its delight in sun, sea and sand.

Thanks perhaps to new-generation Americans, Oxford people tend to wear black over their T-shirts, opting for camouflage or the way black swallows light in cities such as New York. No flash. No pomp, but understatement as street-smart prudence, hoping not to be attacked by a horde of Asian or German tourists, fresh from those open-topped buses that obstruct the ground-level view. Also, all those wannabes wearing Oxford T-shirts aren't Oxonians at all, which makes you wonder why the Oxford magazine touts them, presumably for non-readers, whereas "I READ" might be tribally popular.

The Oxford of today is a glum, sulfuric place, filled with traffic regulations, and anyone peering up at colleges as their spires aspire is likely to get felled. Even in my day (in those days of days), Oxford was noisy and stinky, and it has now degenerated into an ammoniac show-palace calculated to panic any impressionable young scholarship candidate into taking train via Bletchley Junction to the lighter blue, where strolls by the river are still to be had, and views too of the colleges. Newton and Co. have won out in the battle of the Minolta. I think this sad, but how much does sadness motivate you when you are hell-bent on a view of Magdalen and its deer, or Worcester the garden college? Earplugs come in handy, and wrap around glasses to keep out the auto-industrial grit that flies along the High. Oxford has become flamboyant in an out-of-the-body sense, a Frankenstein overlay on the road map of Southern England. The city is full of impotent, raging ghosts to whom the automotive workers who were there in even my day compose an aghast proletariat for whom the academic gravity of the place has slid away like a colossal starship of brain into outer space, where it is quiet enough to go on reading. During the latter part of the week, George Street becomes quite hellish. Inside and out, the pubs flaunt brawny bouncers unknown in my day, and there are police alarms and anti-theft devices everywhere. Such the coveted anathema of a new era that has also seen the Bodleian Library splendidly refurbished and the Ashmolean Museum redesigned and rebuilt. I wonder why those who run things have allowed this muddle. The answer must be money and more money, in whose service there thrive mutants who, with a little better muscle tone, would have become successful anal retentives.

LOOSE CANNONS

I am not much of a party-goer, perhaps because some quirk of my hearing enables me to hear talk from twenty or thirty feet away with discrete clarity, which blots out my interlocutor of the moment, alas. I can be heard all right amid the clamor, but I do not hear what I should, thanks to all sorts of peripheral noise. It was always so, though I seem to have been getting worse.

For a Commem Ball, though, I had to turn out. It ends the academic year with a suitable anti-climax, and all kinds of visitors want to join in, Puffin Blain included, if she could only tear herself away from observing the bouncy-twitchy small rear ends that so impressed her. I was not graduating or anything like it, but many were and the net effect was that of a black hole. You got sucked in, had to rent a tux and bow tie, accommodate the girl of your choice (at the Randolph, this year), and try to dance. I imagined that Commems at other colleges were much more lavish, with titled visitors and even celebs (Silvana Mangano at one, Jean Simmons at another, and so on). We made do with some military types in full dining-in dress, with dwarf medals and lots of twisted golden cord. Parsons in dog collars brightened the scene, as did the best-endowed girls with little smears of talc in their cleavage, which might have been gunpowder instead.

I was always amused by the vigor with which clergymen danced, as if they had been saving it up for the whole year; but then, they weren't celibate anyway, so perhaps they were responding to the generally wholesome air of the whole event. It was safe to let your guard down, or almost so: some girls opened themselves up to intimacy, though the Commem so far as I could gather was in tribute to alcohol, "champers" in particular, and the aim was to get sloshed. The real name of the game until booze took over was talk, and introductions, which soon rendered us hoarse. I thought there would be games, and indeed speeches, but no: swig away and forget the toils of the year. In between bouts of sup, I admired the keenly chiseled lips of Miss Blain, an acute combination of straight lines and oblique angles, giving her a gipsyish look akin to that of Ava Gardner, whom she resembled. File it all under romance. We danced little, then retreated in search of breakfast, which seemed to me the most desirable commodity in the world. But the Randolph, being a British hotel, had its own ideas about that and made us wait. We should have gone and picnicked by the river, as wiser folk did (and on May 1 morning had). And of course sleep intervened.

It would have been different if, instead of their sisters and home-town prom queens, the men had invited the nurses, but not a nurse was to be seen. Then we would have been liberally supplied with breakfast and God knew what other samples of high living. There would have been fewer corsages and more corpses. Even the parsons would not have been safe from the special communions of the stethoscope girls. Oh for their earthiness, I thought, as Puffin B. rattled on through her roster of next destinations, from Calcutta to Montreal. I imagined many a nurse had pleaded to attend, but that would not have been proper, although I was told that Princess Astrid of Norway had popped in briefly to see how the bourgeoisie was doing. I knew now that I would pass up next year's ball and check myself into a neighboring hospital as an emergency, just to see what happened next, even if only breakfast. If anything was for show, this was, and I regretted the fee I'd had to pay just to get in. In the minds of some besotted dons, this event gave the year "closure," to call up that overworked and tedious word. The best part was the champagne and the reappearance of my globe-trotting girl friend, who now worked First Class because she had languages.

What then of the band, that Lawrence Welkish geezer group? I am a devotee of good swing bands, and this was what the occasion demanded, but no Basie, no Goodman, no Herman, no Ellington, no Shaw, no Dorsey. Instead, the old brigade making water into a sleepy lagoon. They must have come cheap. I wouldn't have minded a first-rate chamber group either, at least tinting the background against which we chattered. I don't blame people for not dancing to them; nor did they, like bobby-soxers in the Forties, cluster around the band in mute, inert adoration, as with Goodman and Ellington in particular. I wanted more bounce, more pizzazz, from whatever niche in the halls of music the band occupied. Never was background music so doubly relegated to the hinterland, dancers and non-dancers alike. As I say, being my mother's child, I could have taken the *Goldberg Variations* all night rather than Lawrence's Welkin; but, in truth, the evening and early morning whisked by, talked to death, sheer noise its own victim. A good record-player would have done much better for us, but was not half so suave as an aggregation. Indeed, as the event wore on, I heard rival melodies invading the quad as the gaggle broke up into component parts and the parts got the music they wanted and deserved, so that those of us remaining in the quad tapped heels to several interloping beats.

I got to thinking about our Ball and wondering if, in order to make an impact you remembered years later, the event had to be grossly extraordinary. And ours was not: in fact, just what you might expect. Routine leaves no skidmarks on the *tabula*, not even one that's *rasa*. On the other hand, if you have made whoopee for the past eight weeks, or even for the past three terms, you may be too tired, too uninventive, having left behind you, much like the masterbombers of Bomber Command not that many years ago, a bright and caustic ring of incendiaries to mark the target. Nothing can come up to it, and you perhaps don't want it to. After a year of highs, you need an apocalypse, the word with Calypso entombed inside.

Well, I have a letter here from Lincoln's senior tutor, P. W. Atkins, on Lincoln College Overseas Old Member stationery, a newsletter actually, in which, among other things, he talks about the impending Commem Ball slated for June 29, 1979, to which a double ticket costs thirty pounds, but includes (wait for it):

> dinner with wine, breakfast, a collection of bands, the Cambridge Footlights Revue, a casino, all-night films, a belly dancer, a knife thrower, a helter-skelter...and a string quartet.

Glory be for another generation's Commem Ball! Am I alone in thinking that ours, the first or second postwar generation, had been too much sobered up by war and its austere aftermath? All this time, we thought we had been having fun, and we weren't. Had the ex-servicemen, in all their disjointed seriousness, influenced us too much? It is hard to believe, but it may just have been true that the Zeitgeist had cast a disapproving snoot on us and converted what we thought our high jinks into standard old games. Our high antics lay ahead of us, or would never be. What response would the films, the belly dancer, the knife thrower, have extorted from us during the June beforehand? I will never know, but I have an abiding sense that we were too serious a generation, not a lost one but a staid one, fathered upon anxiety by blitz and loss. Hence, perhaps, my early worries about painful literature as distinct from debonair farce. Too late to delve further into all that now, but seriousness took some of us early, I trust, into the lustrous orbit of serious literature, music, painting. Not a bad if rather stunted and premature initiation. I hit on a concept I have not exactly treasured, but have found fitting: successful sadness, which I found in my supervisor, in Isaiah Berlin (not just for having been mistaken for Irving), in even the cheery, white-haired Dickensian Bateson, my final tutor.

Was this, I used to wonder, what war had done to *them*, as my father's disaster had done something to me, seeing what Thor's sledgehammer could do to any bright potential. If not war, then what? Weren't you supposed to enjoy life? No brilliance daunts death. That must be it. Commem Balls existed to snap you out of it, putting your Kant and Husserl aside for *My Fair Lady*. I found something medieval about Commems, infiltrated as I supposed them to be by somebody's allegory of love. (Not Lewis's.) *Just another dull old hoop*, I hear John Sparrow muttering in the shadows, maybe consoling himself with the renegade thought that, at Oxford, we do to the young what unfits them for those they rashly think their intendeds. We train them to think a little more highly of themselves than they used to. They end up moving mountains, running countries, edging into titles. To be sure, but is that all? The Commem Ball, to the likes of me, is there to surfeit you with childish things, which certain generations need more than others do, to bring them down to earth from the champagne years. We, I guess, started dull, but also grave, and prematurely so. Our *Bohème* was rather stately, replete with images of evil we had never imagined existed in our day and age.

A Big Picnic

Strange how little we noticed the food on offer that evening and morning, perhaps not very tempting. It was already dawning on me how our relationship, Puffin Blain's and mine, left much to be desired, as people say. Eventually consenting to my sexual endeavors, she accepted them with good-humored insouciance as if I were expressing a preference for an aisle seat. How many men had lunged into her while, so to speak, she was engrossed in Somerset Maugham or Lope de Vega? Somehow, everything seemed trivial to her, and I wondered if this was a result of so much top-class service done with practiced reflexes and acquired formulas. We were all customers or clients. Or perhaps it was a deep-seated indifference to me and my peculiar ways: not dancing, always writing, concerned about literary matters. She had always been this way, it was only more extreme nowadays. She had promoted the jocose into an empty lifestyle, and there seemed nothing anyone could do about it, and she really needed someone on her exact wave-length to be at ease with. Not me, I was sure of that. She would soon marry a hearty, jocose pilot, and they would have children of the same disposition, to be admired in the world for their equable good temper, their dislike of nothing.

Our Ball went on, lasting for days perhaps while we scrambled ourselves together and got on with the urgent business of heading for different destinations. As to the food, my mind was a total blank, perhaps an after-effect of too much champagne; if there had been bacon and eggs on the buffet, I could not remember them, or even the aroma of coffee, cocoa, or whatever, and how could we have skipped dinner in the presence of it, steaming and bubbling in huge steel bins? My usually reliable memory was uttering its *non serviam*, as sometimes happened when I failed to recall taking a certain train, announcing myself at somebody's portal, even reading a certain book that obviously had failed to spark my interest. Things as a rule came back to me in excruciating detail even as I tried to be rid of them, afraid perhaps of being snowed under by the superfluous. Commem Balls were for others, that was plain, or maybe in the company of pragmatic nurses accustomed to watching people at their worst in far from their best clothing. *That* must be it. I wanted to get back to my note-scribbling and quasi-academical pondering, to the rhythms of my own mind, best practiced in the dead of night, the blaze or whimper of dawn.

Something else was brewing in the pinball arcade of my head, or rather it had already brewed, something quite different from trying to evolve strategies to manage Puffin Blain's brittle, almost furtive persona. Back in my teens was when it began. All of a sudden, my brain had seemed better wired than usual, and I'd said praise God and pass the ammunition. I now think, many years since that event, this was a consequence of being brainwashed by classical music as a child, nay a babe, for my mother taught incessantly. In those days, I am unsure why, every child had to learn piano (excepting me, of course, who did not want to be part of my mother's mob). It was always piano music, of course, and truly I heard some bungling performers. I also heard the gold medal winners too, plus my mother at her most rallentando, which was exemplary. The piano was in action for as much as ten hours a day, seeding and soothing me (my sister too, who accepted my mother's lovely lessons).

The theory of all this came later, but I am convinced of the link then, at seventeen or so, bearing fruit as I departed from home, thrown on my own resources for the first time, head full of pianoforte classics. The condition abides. I resent not having music to brood or write by. To have it while engaged in my most wayward activities is like being restored to the holy lap of mother earth, perhaps even to the ovary. I was music's child long before I was literature's, or prose's, and I remain palpably grateful for my mother's legacy, laced as it was with her pique that I had gone the other way, not ever learning to read or play music, but with, as she finally recognized, a head full of sonatas. Most writers I know find music and writing mutually inimical, the one tending to mislead the other, but not for me. I need that interior banquet always playing, more and more available as the twentieth century wore on, from 78s to LPs and CDs, as I graduated from concert-going to discs, to an even more intimate setting in which what was interior could raise itself to exponential maximum without the least hindrance. A certain seamlessness invades my mind, balanced, thank heaven, by my mother's exquisite knowledge of grammar, which she imparted to me at her knee, actually handing to me a hard-bound grammar book as soon as I could read, which was early. So, I had both flow and discipline, an amazing pair from an amazing woman. After giving an impromptu lecture at Johns Hopkins, I met a local shrink who confided that I seemed well wired, swarming from one topic to the next without notes, and I told him about my mother's music, and he nodded, he had met the phenomenon before. It was reassuring to know that I could stand and deliver from within the *mêlée* of my thoughts. Lecturing, as often, I always prepared, sometimes voluminously, but I never consulted my notes while talking.

No doubt of it, I was in the right place to get accustomed to these tricks of mind, most of all those almost clandestine dinners at All Souls, the young pharisee invited through the courtesy of my supervisor who, heaven be praised, had had so little practice with students that he just did what seemed the natural thing and invited me to dinner: the civil, civilized, thing to do, and what riches in that vineyard: steady fellows and visiting ones, conspiring at an intellectual ferment of unusual caliber. I was the graft. Carp as I may about Oxford, I will always be grateful for those hours, and that freedom, long enough ago by now to have acquired an unearthly quality, like dining in their desert tent with the inventors of algebra or the devisers of the sky's constellations. What a joy, what an adventure.

It is still hard to tell if this was a typical Oxford escapade or something unique. Did everyone who arrived in Oxford find his/her own way through a thousand shifts to some such awakening? I hoped so. This was the transcendent, invisible, intangible they all kept *talking* about, something tangential and almost accidental that paid you in full for all the frustration you otherwise encountered. It must be true for everyone, I thought, but perhaps they only realized the fact later. And this wasn't some rosy-hued sentimentality of the reconstructed studious era, it was a matter of solid fact and visible proof, yet to me it was as if my bliss at reposing always in the bower of my mother's Beethoven, say, continued straight into those informal gatherings at dinner: nothing in between, although of course there was and always would be. The speed and facility of that continuation, that merging, have always seemed to me magical, carpet or conjurer, as if—forgive me—my mother had wished for it, which I know is corny to think. I just know it was the kind of overflow she would have preferred for me, exactly in line with what she told me at fifteen or so: "You can do anything you want," meaning *achieve*. "Just think it up and do it." I tried to, and became a novelist on a quite different set of keys from hers.

For my twenty-first birthday, my parents gave me a manual typewriter, which I soon mastered, although making the same errors as I make now.

"Now, you're *some* kind of pianist," my mother said, intending some kind of sarcasm.

"Of course he is," my father said, from within one of his wartime reveries. "He's like a Stone Age man with a telescope."

I would attempt sonatas then.

I would bring stars into focus.

They would watch from two hundred miles away.

Improperly held with a slight twisting motion, my typewriter would flex a little, so was it obeying the curvature of space or just revealing its cheapness? Lord Cherwell had the final say. "If space is curved," he said, "in what does it curve?" A conversation-stopper worthy of the High Table at All Souls, where all the tables were High. Lindemann his name. Was not Cherwell the name of Oxford's river? Would there soon be a Lord Isis? Had not even Warden Sparrow, O.B.E., dreamed of becoming Sir John, like Falstaff, or Lord Sparrow, Lord *Passer*? Now I had a clack-clack machine, bane of my father's life during vacations, to fight off Oxford's bells.

My work began to look neater, though surely just as fuzzy in its thought. Poems looked good when typed, but so did envelopes, especially with the return address—"Lincoln College, Oxford" on the front. No postal code in those days, or any other such twaddle.

In the summer of 1950, after graduating, my best male friend and I had gone off to the Italian Lakes by sea and train. What a handsome fellow he was, wavy black hair, flushed Irish coloring, rugger-player's build, he cut a wide swath through the girls. With his cherrywood pipe and resonant voice, he became a familiar figure in the seminar room some of us used. I do believe he was in line to devote himself to philology, an option opened to me also, but I had soured on philology, enjoying Anglo-Saxon and Medieval Literature too much to bury my nose in the mere mechanics of the languages. That in finals he had done less well than I, though much better in philology etc., cast a pall (no pun) over our Italian excursion. He had already arranged to train for a commission in the Army, as a regular, and wasn't exactly looking forward to the fall. We got as far as Lake Como, where we lingered among the deserted hotels, tanning at the lidos where bored-looking servants brought us chocolate and coffee on trays. What a blithe respite it was from all those papers and all that reviewing. Como became our base for excursions to Bellagio and other places, and we toyed with the idea of staying there forever, so cheap and scenic. He swam in the lake while I, unable to swim, watched enviously.

Now news came (it was the beginning of my second year at Oxford) that he had indeed been commissioned in some regiment or other, posted out to Africa, where he contracted TB, and had been shipped home to Midhurst sanatorium in the South. Indeed, the news came tumbling over itself, he had already died.

I took the train to see his parents, who were too devastated to speak; he was only twenty-two, and, as we ignorantly say, the picture of health. "Yes," my mother said, who had met and liked him, "Africa kills them all," referring to young Douglas and pneumonia.

Chastened and sapped, I tried to look after myself as the saying goes, but could find nothing to do except plunge into work. Who would be next? I thought Puffin Blain a likely candidate, but she sparkled off hither and yon with no apparent mishap. We continued to meet, although I sometimes dated her Somerville College friend, Margaret.

With Graham gone, the young were dying first and could not be counted on, and my mind, ever suasible after what war had done to my father, filled with images of the African veldt dotted by exquisitely kempt graves coated with tiny white pebbles that scalded the eye. The main thing, I thought, was to get to twenty-five and stay clear of the military, who kept after us, watching for an angle to exploit.

The death of Graham ("Nutty") Bolton had affected me profoundly. In our day we had sat there in the seminar room, at the table or even on the warm pipes in winter (inviting sterility, one elder told us), just guessing what the future held, imagining the best, of course. Had we gone to Italy earlier, we might even have shaped that threadbare idyll into something grander, turning it into a portent, a seductive illustration of delights in store for two affable young men of literary or philological bent. We knew we were not interested in trash or "tosh" literature. Indeed, working together on our literary magazine had alerted us to the extraordinary generosity of the best publishers, such as Faber and Faber and Chatto and Windus, who plied us with the best review copies and thus kept us in touch, we believed, with the best new things forthcoming. Such was the world we gallantly aimed at, knowing there could be nothing in between us and the best that could be thought or said. We dreamed and fantasized, in the best of possible worlds, looking forward because we had already looked around us and discerned what I had called the invisible riviera of the visible world: something more splendid than ever, if you were twenty, as we soon would be, he tending to find in Goethe, Schiller, and Thomas Mann what I found in the French. I remember, among many others, a novel by Frederic Prokosch, the American, that came in for review (and indeed got it). *Storm and Echo* seemed to us the way literature was going to go, and, although we might later recant this view, we would remain in sympathy with a European-oriented art form—American-European rather than English. Something exotic and flamboyant about Frederic Prokosch stirred us, and we thought we could see the future, his and ours, gleaming just beyond the breakwater of his polished prose. A dreamer's dream, no doubt, but we had firmly taken sides against the plain-prose brigade that dominated English letters. We wanted a literature that revealed the full spectrum of human experience, and from that Graham never had the chance to waver, and I never did.

His life was over so fast it seemed an implosion. There was an absence where he had been, an ever-enlarging space that no longer bore the imprint of his features or even his death mask. I had never imagined such finality except for the brief moment when my mother had motioned me to plant a kiss on the brow of my grandmother lying in state among the polished mahogany and shuntling glass of an upstairs room used mainly, it seemed, as a death chamber.

Would we have remained pals? I think so, unless our tastes were to undergo a sea-change. Once upon a time, no doubt the worse for lack of sleep one winter, we had anticipated graduating and moving on, murmuring in unison, "We have been saved," as we negotiated one of life's hoops after another at no great cost, and therefore equipped for the next trial. Such ignorance, such vainglory, was bliss indeed. We had that old Wordsworthian feeling as about the French Revolution, little sensing the drastic inroads a bacillus or a day of uncommonly bright mental activity might do to or for us. We wholly underestimated chance, what Chaucer called "aventure, or sort, or cas." It would descend on us from on high, clawed and inscrutable, parting us forever and sending me onward into words. Thank God he had his time with girls, a continual shiny summer peopled by helpless beauties who had fallen for him. I had my octaroon, a girl skater with body like best India rubber (the rare kind that erases easily) and treasured his old hand's comment that you could make a satisfactory meal off any part of her. She was malleable-masticable, we said, and a diva on the ice. Neither of us, Graham and I, were advanced Lotharios, running our emotional lives in a spirit of enlightened curiosity, yet not enlightened quite enough; there was something yet to be unleashed upon us, and we sometimes trembled at what might be, but not death, we never thought of that.

Perhaps, being and becoming a rather grave child with an increasing tendency to look on the dark side early, pondering the catastrophe my teen-aged father volunteered for, and the death of my friend, I formed a guarded notion about human fragility. What precarious, easily destroyed creatures we were, so full of blood and water that could easily leak away, leaving behind what earlier writers called the "corse." Later on, when I started to teach, in the time zone of the Viet Nam war, *I* felt my ghosts come back, urging me to do something for the returning veterans, mentally stranded many of them, just like the veterans who had waited and waited, while fighting, to begin their university careers. These were the revenants I'd had to wait for as they sloped back into Oxford and Cambridge, enormously schooled in enormity, but a bit unhinged, deluded, unfamiliar with a world that said blithe things about literature and kept rude, percussive life at a distance. The best I could do, and did, was to steer them to the best war poetry I knew of and just hear them out, sometimes letting them down, at other times managing a breakthrough as they hit on stanzas that expressed for them the devastation of war and the unwelcome return home in store for them. I was meddling too much with death, frustration, thwarting, and grief, but nobody else took much interest in such stuff apart from the young heroes so recently immersed in it. Who at Oxford was writing about war literature of the twentieth century? Nobody that I knew. We were not allowed to. T. E. Lawrence, Wilfred Owen, Siegfried Sassoon, Isaac Rosenberg or Julian Grenfell ("I *adore* war. It is like a big picnic") would have been just the ticket, but they were still taboo in that caravanserai of the antique. It was odd that, confronted with the disasters of our own day (the Korean war, for instance, raging to engulf us if it could), no one was allowed to come to life, or to resurrect the fallen. A huge, styptic silence had enveloped certain studies, and many people were editing texts just to keep their powder dry and not attract the attention of the military who, in the end, brought me back from New York to do my national service.

Oxford has altered much since then, and what I recall—old safety-first attitude as if bombs were still falling—stays with me. You were not supposed to be out in the open lest literary shrapnel got you. It was a postwar inhibition. Yet Oxford was kinder to returning vets of the second war than the United States to its Viet vets, many of whom never achieved the quietus in excelsis their return merited. You see, in my memory I am still trying to welcome my own father, before I am born, from the dreadful war that swamped his youth, and I remain acutely sensitive to his predicament, always to the point of tears, eyeing the young prince denied his true inheritance, and content to be his last-launched torpedo, whatever good that did. I sometimes think that universities, rather than obsessing themselves with textual matters of arid erudition, should open themselves up with programs aimed at victims of the present day, converting them if need be to the literature that will satisfy John Stuart Mill's demand for healing power. This power, often undervalued, needs to be studied in detail, as at certain institutions such as staff colleges and, in the one case I know something about, the US Air Force Academy in Colorado Springs, which has some contact with Oxford. Someone such as Stephen Ambrose has aired this approach, as it were opening up a vast dimension of unrecognized human experience. We cannot do without it. Too much of literature, I think, is taught as if seen from the balcony or up in the gods, as if the bleak terminals it envisions were figures of speech afflicting an alien species merely rumored about. Oh no, death, spoliation, and disease are right on top of us, and too much of everyone's life is an emergency. The specialist in war literature will never have to deal with a dead language, or see the end of his/her chosen corpus, or for that run out of veterans full of pain. The Air Force Academy's magazine, *War, Literature & the Arts*, edited by Donald Anderson, is unique but should be cloned for the superb way it mines and brings to light the incessant literature of warresponse. Until we become a peaceful species, we need such a periodical, much as we may flinch to read some of its offerings, having dismissed the war element in human make-up as trivial or illusory.

My father, as the French say, a *mutilé de guerre*, ended up on the trash-heap of militarism, unwanted and unheralded, with just a few cronies to gather around the village cenotaph or drink with at the pub, remembering grander days. You have to live with such sheer subtraction for years to get the full impact of a life squandered into a finality for which there is no remedy. A devout reader, he was unable to read anything for long after returning, and eventually he found television impossible to watch. In the last analysis, it is government who, ransacking the available manpower and then dumping it once hostilities cease, should take the lead in restoring the wounded and the shell-shocked, as it once did after the first war, although in a clumsy, class-conscious fashion.

All this sailed, somewhat raggedly, through my lovely days in and out of the All Souls dining room, through the raspberry tart and the gas fumes from the hissing fires in the Fellows' rooms, as if T. E. Lawrence had come home to haunt instead of skulking away in the bottom ranks of the RAF.

9

MITRE QUAD

NEXT YEAR

Second-year Michaelmas term has begun its casual, abbreviated tread toward year's end. There never was a Commem Ball other than one so perfect it merits a place in everyone's bumptious album. The weather is cooling, the leaves have begun to fall and drift, generating a faint incongruous tinkle as they travel. Something imminently festive is in the air although Term has only just begun. Everyone says how much older he/she is, which means the summer, that Long Vacation in which all the reading supposedly gets done, has had the effect of progeria. We have almost all come back to join the glum, contained contingent of those foreign students who can never go home to Alpha Centauri. Or are they just putting on a front? At home, my father, whose rituals he dare not change, still takes his seat and faces his plate of eggs with bacon, cockeyedly cutting and pushing to the side of his plate a little symbolic morsel of egg and bacon, one on the right for me, perched just at the upsloping lip, the same on the left for my sister, even though we are both grown-up. We dare alter nothing, flanking him as he parts the Red Sea of the egg. My mother, in much the same mood, is still protesting that, if we all want fish later on, she agrees to cook it, fried in batter, but none for her because she cannot abide the smell. The reek of even fresh fish reaches her even though the freshest fish is not supposed to smell at all. These are permanent rites, parts of the household's lares and penates, as the Romans used to say, and nobody claims any right to change them. *Fush* she calls it, broadening the word in antic tenderness aimed at us, just possibly at the fabric of fish itself so long as it figures in no one else's daily ritual. Nothing ever changes except death, and who knows anything about death?

Oxford knows, where people have been dying for centuries, just as if it were a Derbyshire village that Edith Sitwell has advised you to leave pronto. She is not at the Hall, a few minutes' walk away; she is ill, and I wonder if, wherever she is, Scarborough in Yorkshire or Somewhere In Italy, she has been readjusted into that ghastly face mask to straighten her childhood nose. I do not make my irregular call on her to confirm that the gambit worked, that I am in place where I think I belong, thanks to her stimulus. I have now discovered that Elizabeth Jennings also knows her, if I know her at all, in an entirely different way: meetings in London, tea at some club, and so forth. The woman has more influence than I had thought; she is reaching out from within her mechanical, Procrustean mask to change an entire generation. Elizabeth, I remember, actually lives in Oxford, daughter of a doctor, and thus never budges an inch at term's end.

If I had my way, in all honesty, I would stay in Southfield or college for the vacations too, alongside that little tribe of expatriates, which in Lincoln grows all the time, although our Americans and South Africans, even Australians, seem to vanish, going home or just tripping off to London to view the sights. In my primitive way I go home again, tap base, go up to my third-floor attic to read, where the *Boy's Book of Astronomy* perches atop a stack of the *Boy's Own Paper* (*BOP* to you), in whose pages upper-class boys go through the motions just to show lower-class boys how it should be done. What a class-conscious tribe we are, ever on the *qui vive* for hints.

Away from home, I seem to be adopting roles all the time, aping dons or even scouts, pretending to be T. E. Lawrence or St. Exupéry, "Cobber" Kain, air ace of the recent war, or Edith Sitwell in her facial cage. You can do this, rehearsing personae while trying to "set" your face, and until you do you are Proteus, forever changing, withdrawing and reappearing, whoever else you are. It's all part of the walk-on that being twenty or so requires. You look too young. What a complaint, what a vice! You try to age your face, incising lines of worry or abstract thought, but they don't take, and you are soon back to your *tabula rasa*, mildly amused by the pulpy freshness of your skin, the innocent I-have-not-lived-yet look of your face outside your much more experienced mind. I have an All Souls soul in a look of Blakean innocence, full of allusions, short on experience. Blake, seeing humankind from the center of his own crystal, is not a bad companion to have in public or in private, provided you steer clear of the prophetic books and stick to the lapidary, short poems. Or so says Oxford, ever suspicious of the ragged, verbose visionary.

Cleft for me, I quote, thinking of my India rubber girlfriend, who comes and goes, skating to out-of-town performances I know nothing about. I have come here not to work (that's all done, the reading for the year, done in the Long Vacation), but to renew acquaintance, firming the bonds that bind all the way through this life and the afterlife, so that, come what may, you always have a gaggle of chums in or around London, the navel. I think it works that way for several years after you "go down," a coat-tail effect, a function of the terminal moraine, a long-sustained flicker of intimate affinity because there is no other life than this, and you owe it to yourself not to make mistakes. If this is not "jumping the life to come," in Macbeth's bold phrase, I don't know what is, but of course a huge amount of private and public role-playing has gone into it: the poetry-reading face, in both public arena and the anechoic chamber of the recording studio (we all try both), or the cocktail party circuit, the taking-train-to-London look, the How-Are-You when once again at the Savile Club you encounter your potent host for lunch: J. W. Lambert ("Jack, please"), literary editor of *The Sunday Times*, who will send you lovely new-smelling books for review—Robert Louis Stevenson, Letters of Goethe, honest autobiographies, fighter-pilot memoirs—as if some books had been written just for you as you deliver a second imprimatur, saying yes, let it be printed after all, in the reviewer's ultimate redundancy.

All that, coaxed into being over Brussels sprouts and a slice of turkey. I tootle through London's mannish clubland in a daze of delight, having been taken on, given some kind of a job for the first time. I would have done better to focus on my assigned research, but the competition from the metropolis was too great, and who could resist the allure of being read in several million homes over Sunday breakfast? It also paid the piper now and then.

Now to the bicycle. I have never fathomed how my ten-shilling bike weathered the vacations, perched there in Brasenose Lane next to Lincoln, unstolen even if borrowed, untouchable in some sense, awaiting my return, and then, I presumed, years hence, emitting a sotto voce cry of near-prostitution saying he has gone and left me, take me, I am yours. What a contraption I had become, a thing of fragments, an intermittent Londoner, Oxford student, who took morsels from the rim of his father's plate and bibbed with the best of them at *Isis* parties. It was all coming together, wasn't it? I was becoming a soul, was I not, instead of a scarecrow? Somehow, there seemed no blueprint for the creature I was becoming, which made me seem patchily impromptu, a haphazard loser, except there was, as I saw it, a golden mind supervising operations, an Eisenhower to my commando raids. Perhaps this was how all identities took shape, beginning with a modicum of fragments ultimately adding up to something as impregnable as a saint's chops in a stained-glass window in inconceivable Shropshire. You had to be *some*body, or just a body after all.

I mean as my Sunday editor, Jack Lambert, had a body before he had this tweedy body; he used to be a naval officer and I could see him as such, leaning against the bar in dress uniform, his medal ribbons crammed up high and almost out of sight in the Navy way, not even to make room for wings or a parachute. Now he, I say to myself, who used to be that, has become this. What a lovely parade of selves, much as my supervisor had had: military attaché—what a title, as if he were a suitcase after being a barrister and classical scholar. And then Warden. I was surrounded by accomplished selves, which meant both fully achieved ones and clever ones. It was daunting, and I kept catching myself in the middle of a manual maneuver in order to change it, or even interrupting a smile to crease it downward or promote it into an eyebrows-raised flash of worldly wisdom. *All change*, the call one heard at railway stations as one train emptied out, applied to deportment as well. Do you advance at the crouch or the upright, do you flinch on shaking hands or crowd in upon the other? In the end, these metamorphoses died a natural death among the impromptu bonhomie of All Souls, and I soon began to practice watching people out of sight, as if our talk had exhausted them without their knowing it and, as soon as they turned the corner, they would shrivel up and faint, reduced to dust.

How, I wanted to know, did a Jack Lambert shift from being a naval officer, surely a lieutenant-commander at least with that suave severity of demeanor, to become a literary editor? Big reader? There must be more to it than that, I said, imagining him as one of those Australian convoy spotters in New Guinea or the Marianas who, alone and underfed, used binoculars to watch for Japanese warships in the Forties. To while away the in-between times he read books, scores of them and, though you could see him arriving at his chosen or assigned island with huge bookbag on his back, he could be seen leaving with it empty, he having buried the books on the island for the next man. It made sense. Or he was a maestro of the desert island discs persuasion. Well, they were the same thing, weren't they, the only difference being the lushness of the one, the barrenness of the other.

Never mind, I told myself. Now he's Royal Naval Reserve. He was just like my father at the machine-gun nest, perfectly stocked with Jeffrey Farnol and Sax Rohmer. All warriors read. What had *I* done? I'd sent Lambert an essay of mine, the one from *The Adelphi*, and he'd sent me a book by return mail. *500 words, please. Come and lunch in London*. It was priceless.

A CUP OF TREMBLING

Better, though, is what happens when my mother and father take a day trip to Oxford, leaving early morning and taking a dinnertime train back via Nottingham. They are fitter and more agile than I remember, and I realize they both have been thinned out, my father with his diuretic and my mother deprived of ice cream and Irish stout. It makes a difference, they both declare.

This was in the days when you could poke into and out of funny little corners in Oxford, crowds only near Carfax. So, with taxi and bus, we manage to see Worcester, in some ways the prettiest college although often referred to as "Botany Bay" for being so far away, like the penal colony on an inlet of the Tasman Sea on the eastern coast of New South Wales. We also look at regal Magdalen (the distant deer a hit), Christchurch imposing and with a touch of Buckingham Palace. St. Edmund Hall they find cute as a thimble, and Univ. ("Ah, Attlee!" my father exclaims when he might have said "Shelley") a bit boring. Lincoln, which I save for last, they find the right size, and if anything a little cramped. We shop, sit, stare, and then shop, sit, and stare even more, merely nodding at the Bodleian and the Examination schools where I sometimes attend lectures. Merton we miss, and Balliol too, but Hertford's steeply arched little bridge of Venetian sighs, connecting the old part of college to the new, intrigues them, and my father asks about tunnels between colleges. Not that I remember, no. Surely many surreptitious arrivals and exits could have been managed thus. But isn't there a small tunnel into Teddy Hall from Queen's Lane?

I vow to check on such trivia, more for my own satisfaction than to enlighten my parents, who hardly need to know. We have already begun to play the lunchtime game, the mock-heroic guess at who is in most need of lunch: "Was that me, or you?" Usually me, I tell them, largely because my tummy's mild scowling noises match those of a baby lion. The image is mine, as well as the "blame." I have even imagined that, if you were lucky enough to have a lionet within, that quiescent minor growl is just the sound it would make.

Lunch at the Mitre is extraordinary (this was before the hotel became part of Lincoln College; it had always belonged to Lincoln). After we are seated in a quiet corner, my father excuses himself and doesn't come back. When I excuse myself and go in search, I find him at the bar with some old contemptibles, as we call survivors of my father's war, drinking death and disgrace to the French and Belgians and agreeing that the Germans were a better lot, just on the wrong side for a few years. They have identified him by the wound badge he sometimes wears, although you have to be a keen observer to appraise the dead eye. They are well into their second or third Scotch, and the yarns are flowing; but it is time for lunch. They will be there until closing time, they tell him, two-thirty or so, possibly three, so he vows to return after his lamb chop and fight a few more battles. My mother protests that, no, she too is never lonely when she has food in front of her, and tucks in. They like this restaurant, its chops and steak, and so do I. My mother would love a bottle of stout, especially after inhaling my father's bouquet of Scotch, but she denies herself, and we leave, turn the corner, and again approach Lincoln, next door to Exeter.

No great haste about this, slowed up as we are by a Mitre lunch that is actually a Lincoln lunch (and a Scotch or three), yet there is none of the dawdling that sometimes occurs when the desired object is in view and you have been there before. Here it is, in a college-like street, full of nothing but colleges, ready to let you in or turn you away. Whichever place you have in mind, the entry is simple: pause, step over the lintel of the porter's lodge, and behold the mown lawn, saying who may or may not step on the treasured grass, submit to the hurly-burly of lunchtime, in this case not very tall youths scurrying and exclaiming in narrative laughter. This happens to be one of three colleges on this almost backwater street, which makes it into an approach between quads, more a garden walk than anything because whichever way you go you end up within the sight and smell of short grass, which as we know is one of the more desirable destinations for the human animal. At once the mind grows peaceful, secedes from the fray of figuring and estimating. Even when there is nowhere to sit, there is an oasis, little heeded by the young men within, but at once congenial to the visitor, whose reasons tend to be exaggerated, postponed, and ineffably personal. At once my mother sits down on a bench, hearing as I myself often hear for other reasons the sounds of an organ from elsewhere (the chapel), and being who she is recognizing the sounds of "Jesu, Joy of Man's Desiring" (from Cantata 147: *Herz und Mund und Tat und Leben*), perhaps merely being tested out, yet fortuitously apt. She has found immediate music and immediately lapses, if that be the right word, into a disciplined reverie: someone else is playing for her, and she nods as the performance earns its grade. *Very Good.* An Organ Scholar. My father sits, heeds, makes a sideways motion of his head, and then departs with one of those calming, settle-down motions of his small machine-gunner's hand. Back to the Mitre for however short a session, which really means sitting down with a Scotch and the contemptibles, who if gone will have left an atmosphere behind them. With my mother amiably settled beside Bach, where she so often is, he can let his young mind roam, and, since it is not she who's playing (though organ's in her repertoire, with the village church often asking), he can wander instead of crouching by the closed door to catch every nuance.

"That'll take care of him," she murmurs. "Long-postponed." She is not being cryptic, but merely allusive, as music, where else but in her, subdues the dominant hemisphere of the brain and provides the paradise required. She is luxuriating in this, the one person in the quad seated, and maybe the only one deep in meditation, savoring Oxford life for the second time (her visit two hours earlier was a perfunctory, unseated thing, a touching of base, not bass).

After sitting beside her and clasping her hand in unison, I stand, survey the greensward with a groundsman's eye, and leave her to it a moment, knowing that when she, food, and music compose the trinity there is no need to interfere or even be along. She has this portable peace within her that tells me she is here on the planet for a long, long time, as both guest and music-maker. Part of all its peaceable moments belong to her. I turn away, musing, only to look back at her and see, soignée phantom, a prosperous-looking woman taking a seat beside her, well, in the opposite corner, and pleasantries being exchanged. Who is this, distracting her, at least as I think it. I watch a faltering conversation begin, wobble, then resume with special avidity as something appears to occur to both women: some sudden common ground not music. Frozen to my spot, I grow downward into the turf, knowing it is none of my business. Half-tempted to seek out my father in the trenches, I resist, and gather what I can from earshot, which I am sometimes good at. None of us is part of the lunchtime rush, which avoids the grass as required by little signs posted here and there like one-dimensional shoeboxes. Keep off the grass, property of Gaffer Wordsworth. The chat is of sons, no more than that, but awkward, breathheld, not coming easily as it could have: more explanatory and gestured than tumbling out in the usual course of strangers encountered on a seat. No, this is special stuff, never attempted in speech before, and it has to do with a youth who won his scholarship but never made it to the college of his choice (or the one the examiners assigned him to, since I have no knowledge of how the colleges combine for Classics). How intense and intent, Bach almost shelved in the interests of something graver. Good heavens, what can it be? So it happens to be a lost son, whose absence in the quad this lady has arrived to recognize, no doubt witnessing the uproarious scene he might have joined, the youth on the fringe who is myself: one of those *allowed* to continue, I tell myself. My mother listens, speaks something low, and they both drift into a humbly pensive silence, back to the continuing Bach and the noises-off of young men retreating from yet another curry and, now, Albinoni sobbing.

Then it is over. The woman rises, my mother half-stirs, absorbed in yet another life, and the two women part with figurative bows, no wave of the hand, just an inclination of the head and chest. Something has changed the tune of the afternoon, and now my mother counts on the Bach to see her through. No authority figure has shown up to disarm or disturb, so she is free to mull over her new thoughts, gratitude mingled with empathy, as the woman departs, a galleon among so many skiffs, leaving behind her in the quad an aroma of—what? Mothballs and Chanel? She has not worn that fox fur in many a year.

Her own son, my mother begins without emphasis, and I rejoin with an unvoiced I know. Understood, with no need to say more. I overheard enough and wonder where she came from, almost haunting the place of merriment, not potent enough as a griever to bring the quad to heel to join her in sadness. Does she now go and read *Lycidas*? Mother has had an encounter she will ponder for years: the coincidence, the one woman's track collegeward intersecting with the other's by train and a short stroll. We could not have planned it this well, if well it's been or will become. Something salient, while my father fights his war, has appeared unbidden, oddly private though divulged, and stirring up minds that had not thought of any such thing when setting out, when embarking on the venture of the day. It happened almost unseen, filed away like a playing card unplayed among the pack, certain to be fished out again at some point (who knows?), but made more pregnant intrinsically for having been alluded to in the presence of a stranger. And that young man has had his run in the college of someone else's choice. Who is to say that one of the astute revellers en route to his curry was not his replacement, an almost military term my father might have relished. Will my mother tell him? I doubt it, not for weeks anyway as she soaks up the texture of the day and the suddenness of the Bach and the other son's mother.

Time to bid Lincoln farewell. No bishop intervening. No Rector. Just the troops milling around as my father, pointing at his watch, reappears looking flushed with triumph, amity, and Scotch.

Is it time to rejoin them, he half-implies. No, rejoin *us*, we say, and I show him where to relieve himself, and then we take my mother back to the Mitre to fix herself up. Then we simply take the big red bus to the station and they are soon seated in the dining car, ready for yet another meal northward.

Odd how we skipped Southfield House, as if my mother had felt it was somehow indelicate to invade the quarters of all those young men. She might have enjoyed the peace of the grounds and the remoteness of the big house up that long private walk past the cricket field and Cyril's pavilion, but she might have grown fatigued with an extra bus ride, there and back. My father would have gone along, but puzzled by a visit to the barracks. Two and a half hours later they will be back north where people are bluffer and heartier: not so much finesse or curtseying up there. Not that they found Oxford that demure, as they would have found it in the nineteenth century. Now, if so disposed, they will select their colleges, my mother Lady Margaret Hall, as she has so often said, because it has a melody in it, to it, my father the college named for Ruskin because he sees it, he who knows naught of John Ruskin, as a college for sergeants. She will make any sacrifice for music; he will do almost anything to heed his pundits, whom I remember as Tom Driberg, Hannan Swaffer, and W. Barrington Dalby, two on politics, one on boxing. I would never have consulted them for a flea in my ear, but he does, daily, and who is going to deny him any brush with those who claim to know? He may grouse, claiming he's overworked, but it's all part of his birthright palaver, and he's never going to give it up, even when my mother is giggling about a second choice, St. Hilda's no doubt, destined to become the only women's college still consecrated to women, but she really would prefer LMH, to which one of her music students went.

Odd too not to have visited All Souls, the scene of my encounters, although I wrongly suspect it does not allow visitors, who would disturb the erudite reveries that go on there as big minds cogitate whatever in the total absence of students. Except for me. Some other day we will have to return, making an overnight of it, taking in the two places omitted. I realize I am not a very good tourist guide, or even one to squire parents around. I am best when frozen to the spot watching them bring eyes to bear on things normally beyond their ken. Statues, of savants burned or venerated, do not do much for them, or merely functional buildings in which people do not live. The hotel interests them more than the college, but the lawn more than anything. The whole idea of the quad, enclosed and more or less serene, with all those windows looking down, appeals to them, variant as it is of the enclosed garden. They would like to live on a quad, I think. They would have to wait long years in order to live together in the same college, with the door wide open for tea even then.

ABROAD

I write these words in a large bright mirrored room in the tropics, between a Catholic church and a raucous night club that used to be a sedate Italian restaurant. The street is noisier than it used to be, not with Christian bells, which I have come to relish, but with demolition and then the eateries that replaced the cobbler, the consignment shops, the laundry, the stationery store and the camera shop. Now, in addition to the restaurant-club whose name is a number such as 231 (I have not bothered to memorize it), there is a self-styled Asian place that makes you pay for rice and from which nightly comes the reek of scorched marinated meat. The rest is banks, but right beneath my balcony there's a bike shop and a delightful French bakery that serves a mighty quiche lorraine. It is easy to re-enter the trance of the street-before, which I miss, but easier still to get back the culminating years at Oxford, when I really settled down and worked. At least, when I came back from a year in New York at Columbia (what a contrast), I worked hard so as not to attract the attention of the military, who interviewed me at the Air Ministry as soon as I returned. They were on to me, though, and perversely pleased to see me back, even though Korea was no longer in prospect.

My American friends had talked me into it, out of Oxford into Columbia (I'd asked for Harvard), which was even more exciting. I needed ten references, ranging from Warden Sparrow to Lynn Bartlett, managed to get them, fill out the sheaf of forms, and await the call one way or the other from the American Embassy in Grosvenor Square ("*grosvenor*" surely meant big hunter and I was after big game).

Oxford, however, had become a way of life, in which I could exploit my old-fashioned side, my Ludditism, not that I wanted to become a Fellow of some college (too much teaching); I didn't know what I wanted to do beyond my habitual literary eclecticism, occasional journalism, and my shift as if along a spectrum from poems to essays to, at last, fiction, at which I was working hard, although my first two manuscripts bit the dust—I burned them and was tempted to leap after them into the flames, true suttee fashion. I was becoming pettily learned and wanted to continue until the grand enlightenment came along and swept me up to glory.

When word came that I had been chosen to visit Columbia for a year, I felt exhilarated, yet with somewhat knocking knees. My mother knew gangsters would get me, but my father envied me. He too, at my age, he said, among the Yanks who thought they'd won the war. "Only after 1941," he joshed. "*We* won it up to then."

On my last visit to Grosvenor House, I received in actual dollars my first allowance for New York, which would include a monthly book allowance! My ticket provided steerage, with three others, in the *Mauretania*, a ship that both rolled and pitched, at the same time regaling us with orange ice cream. I was sea-sick for several days, along with many more. John Bowen of St. Anthony's was also on board, headed for Ohio State, as well as Mark Bonham Carter. In fact, it was just about a boatload of students, all en route to some part of the USA, privy to the great adventure that began in the Henry Hudson Hotel on West 57th Street, where we formed a homogeneous group until we scattered, I to the Arizona Motel up by Columbia, right on the airshaft with no air conditioning. It was late August, and I still recall that last night aboard ship, standing at the rail with Jill Tester, discus-thrower from the University of Exeter en route to the College of William and Mary in Virginia, watching the clogged traffic of lower Manhattan swarm by, and then discovering among a multitude of canny things that you could order breakfast simply by uttering a number: "Number Two," and it all came toward you, none of your British "It's off today."

I strolled through Harlem toward Columbia, met Lionel Trilling, and William York Tindall who told me I was too well-educated to spend time in his seminar. "Go and enjoy the city," he told me, "and come by." When I showed up at his apartment, he installed me in what he called "Dylan's chair," where Dylan

Thomas had sat and drunk Scotch. Something disabused and free-and-easy impressed me about this new lifestyle. I moved to a big mouse-infested apartment belonging to one Emily Hahn, not the writer although I kept getting her calls, at 3117 Broadway and spent a week or two getting used to the racket of the subway as it burst up out of the earth to rattle the windows. I had arrived, and it was not Oxford. The area was called Morningside Heights, a joyous name, and the fifteen-cent airmail stamp was green. At some point, to try it out, I moved into 1314 John Jay Hall, but abandoned it, being unable to cook in my tiny room. Thereafter it was a commodious apartment temporarily, assigned to some teaching fellows I had run into, this on Riverside Drive, where I lived on steak, cream cheese and Pabst Blue Ribbon, keeping a long block of steak in the freezer and daily breaking off a chunk to cook. I had been officially enrolled in Comparative Literature and found my way into the Trilling-Barzun seminar (easily forty souls), where I once made a speech about the British political theorist Walter Bagehot. Only Trilling seemed to have heard of him. In between times I went to lectures I did not need to attend, most of all enjoying Gilbert Highet, the Balliol-educated immigrant who also performed on the radio, Mark van Doren, Justin O'Brien and others, showmen all. Two New Yorkers, high-school teachers at Columbia on fellowships, Burton Pollin and Isidor Starr, adopted me and took me to lunch, at which I discovered the variety of American menus and the beauty of New York women.

It was a long way from curry at Lincoln, a kind of squalid-lavish as I perused the city, its subway maps, and collected my living-and-book allowance monthly from the Institute of International Education, and learned how to lurk at International House, up at Columbia. What a good library Low was, with typewriters you could rent for a quarter.

I saw television for the first time and, during the vacation, made a foray south by bus, as far as South Carolina, actually returning by DC-3, for which I had saved up. I thus discovered racism in the South and came back appalled, only to discover the Rosenberg trial and execution. America had teeth, I could tell. They didn't kid around. While I was away, an acquaintance occupied my Broadway apartment. All seemed well when I got back, but the bed was full of dried blood and the refrigerator crammed with beer in amends, I supposed. I had encountered a folkway I hadn't heard about. Nor had Emily Hahn, I guessed.

The year flew by, with another excursion up to Peggy Ashton, in Meriden, Connecticut, she a daughter from my Derbyshire village who had wed an American soldier, thus becoming a GI bride. They lived in the woods of Connecticut in a house he had built with his own hands, picking up terminal moraine rocks to build it with. He was a genuine piece of the frontier, a person of seemingly endless resource, and I admired him. In New York I had discovered my first twenty-four-hour city and I have a treasured memory of arriving back in Manhattan around two in the morning, obliged to take the crosstown shuttle, and encountering in the subway the aroma of fresh-brewed coffee. There appeared to be no rules, but a seamless availability of everything. I had begun to settle in to my first big-city university, living up by Leon's bookstore, where I borrowed from his wide range of French literature (a quarter per week) and taking the local subway downtown to the sights, the museums and the movies (I was often at the *Thalia*, which was nearby). Asking for an extra year, I got it only to have the RAF veto it and demand my return as promised, and the *Queen Elizabeth* took me back to Southampton, a thorough convert to the American way.

Having had my immersion in New York, I could now understand some of the mystification felt by my American friends on arriving in Oxford, with its rundown cafes, its heavy coins, its weird ways of speaking, the lack of TV, rationing, its postwar mentality. No wonder they headed for Brize Norton, the US Air Force base near Oxford, where the PX dispensed home cooking and home comforts, some of which they generously brought to their British cousins. I myself had been just as puzzled as delighted in Manhattan. Now, after witnessing baseball, I understood why cricket confused them, and I took it upon myself to escort several Americans to the longest game in the universe.

PROPAGANDA ANGELS

Returning from the bright cacophony of Manhattan to Oxford's durable halls, I was the addict homing to his drug. Piquant, hectic New York had no peace or quiet save the stern rattle of a commercial enterprise by whose standards Oxford's car factories were minor and sedate. Now the bells, wonderful to say, diffused serenity and rural charm, almost like the rippling gladsome bells that preceded the six o'clock news on the BBC: an aural resumption of peacetime calm (during the war, no bells rang; had they done so, it would have been to announce Nazi paratroopers floating down like *gummipuppen*). After the hassles of even Columbia, Oxford was a haven of Victorian quiet, and its bells proclaimed, I fancied, the descent of propaganda angels in whom I did not believe but accepted as a light militia of the lower air. I had missed complacent England for a year, and its ritual offerings.

No more of my octaroon skater, gone the way of best India rubber. Gone too Puffin Blain, taskmistress of busy behinds all sequestered, I hoped, in some microcallipygous zoo. I took train via Leicester to an Oxford that was between terms, and strangely monotone with no sudden surges of the student body as lectures ended and bicycles whirred again. Our two Welsh sisters were still there, though, on the qui vive for Lincoln men on the loose, especially those wearing drainpipe pants, which were still the rage, I had no idea why, but I smiled at the flimsiness and mindless avidity of the infatuation. I felt like some beast from the ancient Egyptian ritual of the cattle count. My pants were baggy and American. At Columbia, just before I left, a lovely girl of Russian origin had confided to me that I had been known to the Trilling-Barzun seminar as "lovely young Hamlet," which chastened me no end. I still looked too young, too defenseless, for my breeches. I could now see why the faculty, having observed me, judged I didn't look old or tough enough to teach. Indeed, I more and more resembled, my mother said, her brother Douglas, who certainly had never looked old enough to die. To acquire a nickname I'd had to sail steerage three thousand miles. Back now, I was my own self again, with a degree in comparative literature from an exotic place. In the old days, I'd heard, they wrote it A.M., but now it was M.A., altogether more conventional, but concealing a love of far-out literature.

Southfield House was empty, but the ground-floor windows were open to summer's bouquet and, I supposed, itinerant bats. I clambered in for a merely atmospheric, nighttime check, clandestine but definitive. It was Owen Harries's old room, bookless and stale, but all kinds of conversations, from what seemed eons ago, came back and whirled around my brain. How very much we had all talked and talked, educating ourselves without knowing it. Less intrusively I began to stop by the public library to call on Elizabeth Jennings, whom I saw in after-years in hospital, the worse for wear after a crisis, with jam and bread-crumbs on her mouth, still writing of course and, as it were, tunneling her way through the slough of something or other, always into succinct stanzas loaded with her special rhythm.

A small book of my essays had appeared while I was out of the country, and one day a much-forwarded letter showed up from C. S. Lewis of Magdalen no less, taking my points seriously one after another and then advancing to outright self-expression on the pain of losing his American wife to cancer (the subject of subsequent movies). I was moved and astounded, and, reading between the lines of Lewis's letter, divined the distress afflicting his faith. Somehow he managed to keep it, but by a chain of reasoning I found hard to accept, even though he offered this candid letter to show just how a man up against it could manage things. A real *mensch*: such was my verdict on Lewis, writing to a stranger from the thick of things. His problem of pain remained, the believer still half-doubtful, the non-believer indignant. Had I signed up for medieval or Renaissance literature, he and I might have had some further talk, but I kept clear of his disaster. I wondered how many dons would have written such a letter. I had heard about Lewis's teaching that he took gravely the opinions of just about anybody, either to make them feel good or to engage in severe Socratic elenchus. His grim aplomb drew crowds who wanted to see where the discussion would end up. That his dying wife was American made him stand out even more; she had been given some funny looks in Oxford as visitor, intended, and wife. And "furriner." Shame on them.

I no longer dined at All Souls, a college with which Freddy Bateson had no contact, and not much more even at Corpus, his own slowcoach place. Instead, we lunched at one or other of Oxford's grimmer cafés, eating abstractedly to the rhythm of ideas. Only rarely was it the pretentiously named Taj Mahal, whose delights were caustic but left Freddy unmoved and unburned. Little did he care that, when we could afford it, we spiced ourselves up at the Taj. Gruel and sago pudding would have pleased him just as much. It was like trekking through no man's land, with all friends gone, a change of the old order and a certain freedom attained, but I kept up my visits even while in the RAF, though never in uniform, which prompted Bateson to joke that I wasn't in the military at all but an American spy.

I have by me a seating plan from the All Souls Encaenia Luncheon of 23rd June 1999, with just a few of the old names upon it: Lady Berlin and Professor Hampshire. Too many gone. After all, it was fifty years ago that I became a welcomed trespasser. Essentially, Encaenia is when Fellows get to return kindnesses and to encounter distinguished other guests. It has little of the secret society about it, more of the stationary garden party. To study the seating plan with any memory at all is a bit like a sequence in a movie when someone hands his card to someone else, and the next frame, seamless and adroit, reveals a third person's hand receiving it. The postcard-sized menu, with no mention of All Souls on it of course but the college mallard in unembossed gold evincing it, offers Salmon Trout with Marinated Cucumber Salsa, followed by Poussin with Julienned Vegetables, then Salad, and Jellied Terrine of Raspberries and Mangoes. The wine is a Montagny la Grande Roche 1996. All very skimpy, I thought, envisioning the luncheon at a distance. No Sparrow with his Tom Conti looks, his habitual double-breasted suit, its way of enclosing the body perhaps a leftover from the army, and one of his many khaki shirts not worn out in the service.

I missed his delicate introductory voice, presenting me at first as if I were some mutant between orphan and changeling. I missed his casual discretion, his openness with his things, his "stuff," as if what he owned was only slightly his and belonged to the college much as Pepys's library did to Magdalene College, Cambridge. No sound of his common question, "Do you like children, Paul?" he little knowing that, in airports and train stations, children come up to me, recognizing one of their own in my glazed, print-haunted stare. Scanning the names of the politicos at Encaenia, I wondered that so few of them ever showed up at dinner, at that august High Table with no undergraduates below it. Clearly, my glimpse of Ali Baba's cave has lingered long, perhaps even steering me toward what I went to Oxford to develop, which makes me sound like the pragmatic, systematic person I am not. My remaining impression of the Warden-to-be was of his loneliness. His chairs and sofas were piled high with books doing duty for people. Arrayed in his bedroom, his few shoes awaited the call, perhaps the loneliest sight in the world, and worst after his death. His rooms breathed gas, smacked of gas, as they say, and perhaps soothed him with ceaseless supply as he sat with Forrest Reid's children perched on his knee. Then the Warden became more palatial, downstairs, with an imposing door that opened on the High, enabling him to bypass the porter's lodge, no longer for a Wolverhampton or London trip stepping into a nearby candy-shop to cash a check for the fare. His letters I saved as icons of flamboyant erudition, and his books of Latin epitaphs as what the soldier Lord Wavell called an anthology of his: other men's flowers. In another day and age, might he have been burned at the stake? No, he was better connected than that, but so were, they thought, Bishops Cranmer, Latimer, and Ridley.

I wondered at the evident austerity of his rooms. No flowers. No coffee-maker. Not even a nail file or a pair of tiny scissors. No bottles of liquor. I liked him to be there for me, but I revelled in his anticipation of summer in Venice, whatever the reality was, whoever was there to be resumed. Perhaps, when he died, a sweet savor rose from him, the holy peptic aroma of good intentions, with which he was liberally supplied, whatever demons or furies tagged on to him, daring him to climb ever higher while, as they say in the

Air Force, keeping an eye on his six. What I ended up owing him remains unpayable.

News of old Oxford colleagues comes in all the time. Elizabeth Jennings ended up at Chatto and Windus for a while, editing with C. Day Lewis. Peter Dale Scott and I have a publisher in common. Martin-Seymour Smith does an occasional review for *The Washington Post*, long a stamping-ground of mine. Derwent May of Lincoln, and yet another novelist, joined *The Listener* and *The Times Literary Supplement*. Wilfrid Sheed, last heard of in Key West, turned to writing about boxing. Bud Stanton served as chair, Agricultural Economics, at Cornell. A poem by Jenny Joseph becomes the *cri de coeur* of the Red Hat Society, a gaggle of liberated females achieving a certain age. Donald Hall survives pain of his own, and remembers, as does the increasingly professional Steiner, whose Hitler novel I have read. Too many, however, have sunk without trace, or indeed risen without it, Lincoln men and others, and some are no more: already no more, like Coutts, cricketer and geographer, housemaster at Oundle School, dead at 69, the first of a generation. I relish a small platoon of learned loyal friends, expatriates in the main, who keep in regular touch, which is important in this vast, irregular, inconsistent continent. Some miss the cricket, and some don't. Some regularly revisit Oxford and some daren't. I find myself remembering my Oxford as if I were there, had been bewitched there, in the sixteenth century.

I am eating wild boar at Christmas in 1524. This is the flesh called brawn, either fashioned into a collared head or made into a jellied terrene. It is what we sometimes ate in my childhood. Brawn is brain, of course, but also strength. The cooking vessels have been scoured by Cranaway, using mainly sand: two shillings and sixpence, plus sixpence for sand. To fuel the fires, a little charcoal and wood aplenty; Robert Smythe has accepted ten pence for timber lugged from Littlemore to the college: "ii treys to the fyre against Chistenmasse," and Felwell gets an undisclosed sum for "sawyng a great tree in pessis to the hall." Candles galore, priced at two shillings and eight pence. The boar has been brought here by the tenant of the college farm at Chalgrove. After slaughter, they tie up the flesh with cord and cloth, then seethe it in small ale. Four pence for eight gallons of penny ale "to be sowsing drinke for the brawne." Cloths and bonds for the seething, four pence. The Bursar receives ten pence for going to Abingdon for brawn, the cost eleven shillings. The price of buying and butchering is always going up, and the college's other tenants have brought capons and rabbits (12 pence) as well as wine (Jerome Westall, 4 pence). On the Eve, the Fellows wash down their brawn with wine (*pro vino in die Nativitatis domini in prandio*), on the Day they take a pottle of muskadell and a pottle of claret wine. Or strong ale. It will not soon be another century. Fellows in residence receive an extra eight pence for their Christmas Commons, and have a goodly tuck-in, games after dinner by the hall fire kept ablaze with extra charcoal. One chorister impersonating a boy bishop for lack of a visitation. This joyous evening, we entertain the Regius Professor of Hebrew, Dr. Bruarne, and Mr. Richard Caldwell, Student of Christ Church, who play tag with us, chasing each other around the troughed-on board as the fattened firelight catches the ivy and the holly in a wholesome glitter.

After the passing of yet another year of bleak triviality and soft grandiosity, Christmas comes again with the arrival at the college gate of the parish clerk and the choir of nearby All Saints Church, on the feast-day of St. Nicholas, 6 December. A refection of wine follows. We pay the parish clerk sixpence for his trouble. "Wyne, ale, and breyd" for Sanct Nicoleys nyghte cost sixpence. A fortnight later, on 22 December, the fellows gather to audit the accounts and then feast St. Thomas with high splendour in the Rector's chamber, more lately known as the Beckington Room.

And always the cry for more candles and lamps, even in the quadrangles and on the stair landings, as our overburdened eyes weaken and wobble before giving up the ghost.

ACKNOWLEDGMENTS

Many thanks to the Reardons for plying me with tapes and vignettes all the way from France, when they had much better things to do. The book is theirs in many ways. When Oxford stymies you, ask a Cambridge man. Ariada Mencken read the first draft and made some valuable suggestions. When Oxford stymies you again, ask a Cornellian. Sheila Forster guided me in the matter of early-Fifties shampoos, and Professor Bill Forster fed me other winning esoterica. Herbert Leibowitz of *Parnassus* emboldened me with his early enthusiasm. Jim McCue of the London *Times* kindly provided me with useful and thoughtful materials, including *pensées* about Winchester College and John Sparrow that I found most enlightening. Stephen Gill, Professor of English Literature and Tutor in English Literature, Lincoln College, kindly answered some vexing questions about the identity of some of my contemporaries, and the Reverend Doctor Vivian Green generously authorized me to make use of his sparkling essay "Christmas in Tudor Lincoln," published in *The Lincoln College Record* (1984-5). One query, about a young playwright of my day, produced no word about him from his publishers, prompting me to take to heart again Broch's phrase, "the immensity of the here and now." Several old friends and acquaintances appear in the preceding pages; for any errors I alone am responsible.